NEGRO WEEK

AT THE NEW YORK WORLD'S FAIR

JULY 23, 1940 – JULY 28. 1940

by

ROBERT LIVINGSTON

TABLE OF CONTENTS

DEDICATION

To all the Black families who attended Negro Week
at the New York World's Fair in 1940.

PROLOGUE

Contrary to what many people believe, history is not an objective discipline bereft of biases that merely studies the facts of a dead past. More to the point, it is a subjective study of the living past requiring an evolving review of events that have influenced the present. That being the case the study of history is influenced by contemporary questions as posed by each generation of scholars. Because of this the study of the past tells us a great deal about ourselves. Our study of the past reflects our contemporary, yet temporal values and perspectives. Since this is the case the study of the past is not a straight line, a linear rope from the past to the present, an arbitrarily and sequentially driven recitation. Rather, history is more like a circle or perhaps a spiral. We are not separated from past events. We are bound to them. What does all this add up to? The study of the past is the search for truth. This is an unending effort and quite different than claiming that truth has been discovered. A skeptical mind knows that historical truth changes over time as new information and events lead to new questions and understandings.

Since the 1960's there has been an expanded effort to rediscover the lost histories of Black Americans, perhaps prompted by civil rights activists. As a group they challenged our accepted views of Blacks in American society, both present and past. In doing so they are altering our understanding of what took place. In short, our prevailing racial stereotypical notions are challenged, as is the view that Blacks quietly accepted their inferior status and second-class citizenship. Nothing could be further from the truth. In the story that follows, Augusta Savage struggles against racial discrimination and the painful bigotry that punctuated her life as a Black artist of considerable talent and achievement seeking success in a white world. Perhaps because of the fickle fates she is commissioned to provide a sculpture celebrating Black cultural life for the 1939-1940 New York World's Fair. There she meets a fictitious Black family that is attending the Fair during what is called Negro Week, July 23rd through July 28th in 1940. Together they experience the wonders of the Fair, even as a myriad of difficult racial questions challenged them. Their story, placed in the past, unearths disquieting attitudes and perceptions still troubling our society today.

CHAPTER 1 – NEW FRIENDS

EARLY MARCH 1962 – NEW YORK CITY

My name is Augusta Savage and I have a story to tell about a very special family that wandered into my life many years ago. If you haven't heard of me, that's okay. I'm not what you would call a household name in most quarters. It's true my sculptures have received some critical acclaim in the art world, as has my school for youthful artists just beginning their work on canvas, or with wet clay in their hands. Now, as to the folks I'm going to tell you about, they also can make no claim to fame. Just ordinary people who decided to take an outing and found their way into my heart way back in 1940. To be more exact I met the Freeman family on July 23, 1940 on a chilly Tuesday morning in Flushing Meadows during the 1939-1940 New York World's Fair. We met in front of my artistic contribution to the Fair. I was making sure that all was in order when visitors assembled to admire what was popularly know as The Harp.

THE HARP   *AUGUSTA SAVAGE*

Whether it was serendipity or the gods weaving a tale for their own amusement our meeting began a lasting friendship. Though I'm in my seventieth year and in declining health I can still see their faces on that first day of Negro Week at the New York World's Fair.

WORLD'S FAIR POSTERS

DAY 1 - JULY 23, 1940

Mr. Abraham Freeman was a husky, very muscular man with a bright smile and a charming baritone voice. At the time he was 55 and a truck driver for the city of New York. He collected rubbish each day with a cheerful glee in his eye because he was a lucky guy and he knew it. The lingering pain of the Great Depression still hovered over the country and he had a steady job, a modest paycheck, and, if he could last another ten years, an even more modest pension. He was determined to do that. He and his family lived a middle class life in Harlem in a tight little framed home that was nearly mortgage free. He was by all accounts a family man with a sharp tongue when it came to keeping his children on the straight and narrow. That was especially true of his son, James, who, unlike his older sisters, tested the limits of fatherly patience. That said he realized he was doing okay for a Black man who could trace his lineage back to slave days in South Carolina.

His wife was Mary Elizabeth Freeman. She was a devout Christian lady and a devoted member of the New York's Urban League where she advocated for social and economic justice. Five years younger than her husband she was a robust, charming person who corralled her children in a manner befitting a third-grade schoolteacher at Public School 77. Unlike her husband who never had a chance to finish high school she had attended Howard University in Washington D.C. There she majored in American Literature and received an elementary school teaching credential. She taught the little ones the three "R's" with a firm hand and a generous smile. But most of all she loved teaching music. That was her forte. Provide her with a piano and she was halfway to heaven.

As you might surmise the Freemans placed a high value on education and expected their children to excel in their studies. They brooked no contrary effort. It was understood in the Freeman household that education was the magic carpet for Blacks seeking economic advancement in the face of the prevailing racial attitudes, even in somewhat progressive New York City.

It was my good fortune to meet their three children. Martha was the oldest, about 23, and like her mother she attended Howard with thoughts of being a high school teacher. English was her thing and Shakespeare was her love. She was tall and strikingly beautiful. Next in line was Rachel. She had just turned eighteen and was attending a local community college. Not as tall as her sister but equally lovely, her strength was math. She had dreams of starting a small business someday once she completed a major in Economics at New York City College. Both daughters were athletic and attractive and always under the watchful gaze of their father who invariably met their dates with a glaring eye and a few straightforward questions. "You'll be home by eleven o'clock? Where are you going again?" Their mother was a little more accommodating. She checked out grooming, diction, and manners. As the girls left on dates she always said, "And have a good time." Last of the brood was James, an inquisitive junior in high school with an aptitude for science and rebounding on the basketball court. James was already over 6'3" and still growing. He was a handsome young man with a dazzling smile that charmed the most reluctant young ladies in his classes. As to his future… Dunking a basketball just might be his ticket to a scholarship at Columbia if he added a couple of inches and continued to hit the books. Perhaps because he was the "baby of the family" and the only boy his parents kept a very watchful eye on him. Keeping James focused was an ongoing task in a town where many a young man easily went astray.

The Freeman family could trace their roots back to West Africa and the tribal freedom they once enjoyed on the Dark Continent before the slave ships appeared on the horizon. Seared into their collective ancestral memory was the cruel passage from their homeland to the painful auction block in Charleston where children were torn from their families, and husbands and wives savagely separated.

THE AUCTION BLOCK IN CHARLESTON

Also embedded in their memories was the harsh plantation life of a slave working long hours under the brutally hot sun and the occasional violence of the leather whip commanding absolute compliance to their masters. Mr. Freeman could trace the migrant history of his elders, first in South Carolina, later in Virginia, and finally in Maryland on the eve of the Civil War. At least three times owners sold his family members to others at a profit, each time driving the forced labor further northward. It was just after President Lincoln's Emancipation Proclamation that Mr. Freeman's great-grandparents met on a dusty road just south of Baltimore as they followed a line of Union soldiers offering food and shelter, and some protection from diehard Confederates. Mrs. Freeman's background was somewhat more clouded.

It appears her great-grandparents were found hiding in a weathered shed by federal troops in Virginia and immediately declared contraband by the officer in charge. Apparently they caught on as camp cooks and as menders of Union uniforms.

Unable to read and write all these former slaves vowed their children would not be afflicted by this painful curse. Over time the two family lines migrated even more northward, always seeking better circumstances. Eventually they settled in New York City, where Abraham and Elizabeth met in a former Dutch enclave known as Harlem.

Important Proclamation by the President.

THE SLAVES OF REBELS PRO-CLAIMED FREE.

BY THE PRESIDENT OF THE UNITED STATES OF AMERICA:

A PROCLAMATION.

I, Abraham Lincoln, President of the United States of America, and Commander-in-chief of the army and navy thereof, do hereby proclaim and declare that hereafter, as heretofore, the war will be prosecuted for the object of practically restoring the constitutional relations between the United States and each of the States and the people thereof, in which States that relation is or may be suspended or disturbed.

When I first met the family I almost immediately queried them about two things. First, why hadn't they visited the Fair the previous year when it opened on April 30, 1939? Second, why had they waited over a year before finally purchasing an attendance pass for one week? To the first question Mr. Freeman was direct. "Cash," he said. "The family simply couldn't afford the tab." He candidly pointed out a few things that explained all. I must admit I was only somewhat aware of the numbers he shared with me.

"The average wage in 1939 was .45 cents per hour for whites and .30 cents for Blacks," he remarked with a wisp of anger. "The average yearly income across the country was $1,368. True the cost of a loaf of bread was only .10 cents, a gallon of milk was .23 cents, and a dozen eggs cost .18 cents, but that still called for ready cash. A cup of coffee costs a nickel and you could see Gone With the Wind for a quarter, and a gallon of gas only cost a dime, but rent averaged about $28 per month." He then pointed out the obvious. "For a family it took $20 each day to enter the park and see all the attractions, as well as to eat. And that didn't include transportation."

"Still, you're here a year later," I pointed out.

"True enough. We made a family decision to do so in the following year. My wife pushed that."

"I did. I wanted my children to see all the exhibits and especially the new inventions being showcased. I especially wanted my daughters to see the artistic and musical displays and events. James was keen to see the technological marvels."

"And that's why we are here looking at your wonderful work. We wanted to see The Harp," Rachel said. "We had heard so much about it."

"You'll tell us about it?" Martha asked.

"Of course."

"And I wanted to see the amusement park," James quickly added. "It just worked out that The Harp was in this area."

"You intend to ride on those scary things, twirling around at high speed, being scared to death, James?"

"You bet," he responded with the verve of the young, always ready to challenge the thrilling and daring.

"Our family decided to save every penny for the Fair, assuming it continued another year," Martha pointed out. "This we did."

"And don't forget what Dad did," James said in an admiring voice. "He worked double shifts as often as possible to save for a weeks' ticket."

"For the family it meant purchasing less of this, not doing that, and always watching the large Mason jar slowly fill up."

"It was worth it, Rachel?"

"Oh, yes," she said, a glorious smile attending her almost musical voice. "Mother and father were determined. Their enthusiasm rubbed off on us."

I couldn't help but be taken by the Freeman family. In many ways they countered a void in my own life: they had strong, supportive family ties, obvious love and affection, and a sense of self-worth to counter racist challenges they often dealt with. Though I did not fully appreciate it at the time the Freemans would quietly become my surrogate family. In this I would receive them with a warm heart.

As to the second question..."Why today" I had asked. Mrs. Freeman piped in without hesitation. "There was little in the fair in 1939 to celebrate American Blacks and our contributions to the country or New York City. It was like we didn't exist," she added stolidly. "So why attend?"

"It was a white man's World's Fair, almost exclusively," Rachel said emphatically.

"What changed your mind?"

"We heard about a program that would highlight the contributions of Blacks to American culture. There would be festivals, exhibitions, song and dance recitals, choral and symphonic music, concerts, and religious services. We couldn't pass up that opportunity to celebrate our heritage."

"You're referring to Negro Week?"

"Yes, Mrs. Savage."

"Augusta, please."

At this moment Mrs. Freeman now asked me a question for which I had no immediate answer

"Augusta, did you know that initially Negro Week was not an official part of the World's Fair program?"

"No."

"Attendance during the first year of the Fair, I've been told, was less than expected and even fewer visitors this year. There was a need to attract more folks. One way was to encourage Blacks to attend."

"You know this because?"

"The Black press informed its readers. It also pointed out that the country was gearing up for war. Civilians were being drafted. Young Black men would be part of the military buildup. There was a need to quiet racial animosities and to unite the country for what was ahead. In the minds of the Fair Corporation Negro Week at the World's Fair was what might accomplish this."

"I had no idea. But again, you're here."

"And we were finally getting an opportunity to end the stupid, dehumanizing myths about Black people as indolent and uncivilized," Rachel interrupted, almost shouting.

"And one more thing, Augusta."

"James?"

"To end the crazy fantasy that Black tenant farmers and sharecroppers enjoyed their lives in the Jim Crow South."

"Where did you learn that?"

"I've got a history teacher who points out things not in the textbook."

"And we wanted to know about folks who didn't always get a fair shake in the white press."

"You're speaking of whom, Mrs. Freeman?"

"I think we could start with George Washington Carver. Did you know he discovered over 300 industrial uses for the peanut? And what about Dr. Daniel Hall Williams who performed one of the first successful open-heart surgeries? Add Richard Wright to the list. His novel *Native Son* was the first work of a Black author selected by the Book of the Month Club. His depiction of discrimination and segregation in Northern urban areas hit home."

"What about Marian Anderson?" Martha vigorously interjected. "Didn't Arturo Toscanini say she had the voice of the century?"

"Add W.C. Handy to the list," Mr. Freeman suggested with a glint in his eye. "No 'blues' without him."

W.C. HANDY   MARIAN ANDERSON

I had to admit I knew little of these people and their accomplishments. Caught up in my own world I was often insulated from what was taking place around me. The Freeman family was reminding me to come out of my self-imposed cloister of wet plaster and thick, red clay. Given my proclivity for total absorption when working on a project that was going to be a real challenge. These thoughts I kept to myself.

DR. DANIEL WILLIAMS   RICHARD WRIGHT

My new friends were providing me with an unanticipated education. Admittedly, they had caught me somewhat off guard. And this led to a new understanding. Though millions of people would attend the World's Fair, Black families would make up only a tiny fraction of those passing through the turnstiles. And then another realization dawned. Racial issues, though always present, yet often muted, were a cloud hovering over the New York World Fair in 1939.

BLACK VISITORS TO THE FAIR *A STEREOTYPE*

A POPULAR POSTCARD

Questions asked and answered. It was time to move on and that meant explaining to my new friends all about The Harp.

CHAPTER 2 – A SCULPTURE OF THE HEART

FAIR FACTS

. The 1939 New York World's Fair season ran for 185 days from April 30th to October 31st.
. The 1940 season ran from May 11th to October 27th, a total of 170 days.
. The paid attendance in 1939 was 25,817,265.
. The paid attendance in 1940 was 19,138,732.
. 52 nations and 11 colonies participated in the World's Fair in 1939.
. Only 44 nations participated in 1940.
. The total operating cost for the two years was $67,010,989.
. The total Fair loss was $18,000,000.
. The total physical acreage involved in Flushing Meadows, Queens, New York City was 1216.5 acres.
. A full price adult ticket cost $.75 cents in 1939.
. A ticket for children ages 3-14 cost $.25.
. A season pass for adults cost $15.00. A pass for children was $5.00.
. The first ticket was sold to Fiorello LaGuardia, the Mayor of New York City, by Grover Whalen, the Fair's President.

FAIR PRESIDENT WHALEN AND MAYOR LAGUARDIA

Putting on the New York World's Fair demanded close collaboration between private investors and local, state, and federal levels of government in addition to the assistance of foreign nations. By way of example, New York City provided $26.7 million dollars. The legislators in Albany contributed $6.2 million. The federal government was in for $3 million. Overall $30 million was spent by foreign nations to build and maintain their various venues. Even with all this, additional funding was needed. The Fair issued $27,829,500 in bonds, which were backed by anticipated receipts from admissions, rentals, concessionaires and exhibitors. The yield on the bonds was a hefty 4% due in 1941. The bonds were sold to businesses, wealthy individuals, and members of the general public. All hoped to realize a nice profit on their investment.

—————————————————

Already a number of people were gazing at *The Harp* even as the Freeman family gathered in a close circle next to Augusta Savage. Of course, it was problematic as to whether any of the patrons recognized her as the sculptor. Since most Blacks hired for the Fair were custodians, gardeners, or helpers in the food outlets this was a reasonable, if not stereotypical view to take. Unless they had seen a photograph of Augusta Savage, onlookers would not make the connection. In any event a common refrain from those viewing the work was, "Now, isn't that something." They were more right than they knew.

THE HARP

"Augusta, why did you call your sculpture *The Harp*?"

"As to the name, Martha…"

"Yes."

"That's what the critics called it and it caught on with the public. I originally called it *Lift Every Voice and Sing*. I took for my theme the Negro national anthem based on a poem written by the late James Weldon Johnson, and set to music by his brother, John Rosamond Johnson. That seemed appropriate since I was a friend of James and understood the message of his inspiring words. I had an opportunity to bring his imagery to life. Fortunately, I was one of four women who received a professional commission (and a $350 fee) from the Board of Design to be included in the Fair. My task was to promote Negro arts and the Negro community."

JAMES WELDON JOHNSON   JOHN ROSAMOND JOHNSON

"Mother, why are you smiling?'

"Rachel, don't you remember? The words I read so often to you and your sister and James?"

Lift every voice and sing
'Til earth and heaven ring,
Ring with the harmonies of Liberty;
Let our rejoicing rise
High as the listening skies,
Let it resound loud as the rolling sea.
Sing a song full of the faith that the dark past has taught us,

Sing a song full of the hope that the present has brought us.
Facing the rising sun of our new day begun,
Let us march on till victory is won.

Though those around them viewing *The Harp* jostled here and there for a better view or a quick Kodak camera moment if they had such a device, the Freeman family remained quiet, permitting the almost mystic words to carry them forth to an anticipated world not yet present.

Facing the rising sun of our new day begun,
Let us march on till victory is won.

"Augusta, how did you come up with this design?"
"You are an inquisitive young man, James."
"That's what my father often says."
"Well then…First, I had little money for the project. I had to use fragile but cheap plaster or clay for the 16-foot tall sculpture. I always wanted to cast the work in bronze but that was so expensive. So much more sturdy…Given the size of the project I had to work on the Fair grounds. It was difficult but rewarding work.

AUGUSTA SAVAGE AT WORK

"People seemed to have many interpretations of your work."

"They do, Rachel."

"But?"

"They often just see Black figures lined up. What I depicted…
What I wanted to depict was a young Black man holding a bar of music
and twelve Black singers representing strings on a harp. The stylized
figures of young Black youths were placed in graduated heights. They,
of course, represented the strings on a harp. The sounding board of the
work was symbolic of the hand of God. Not many visitors, I'm afraid,
saw that deeply into the sculpture."

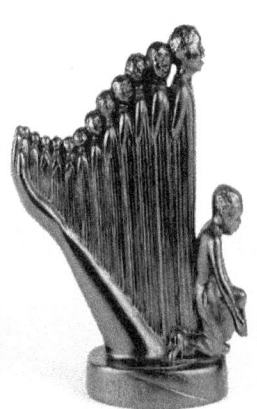

MODELS OF THE HARP SOLD AT THE FAIR

"It's so beautiful. It should be placed in a museum after the Fair
ends."

"That would also be my hope, Martha."

"Will you be able to find a home for your work, Augusta?"

"I'm not sure. It would take a great deal of money to preserve
the sculpture, Mr. Freeman. Bronze is expensive."

"What a terrible loss if it is lost to others."

"I feel the same way, Rachel, but there is nothing I can do. No
museum has stepped into the picture. No philanthropist has come forth.
Still, I will be left with memories."

"As will we," Martha responded. "As will we."

FAIR FACTS

. Augusta Savage did not have the funds to move *The Harp* or to store it following the close of the Fair.
. Almost all buildings and works of art were destroyed after the World's Fair closed in late 1940.
. The Fair was meant to be temporary and ephemeral.
. Small metal souvenir copies of The Harp were sold.
. Approximately 5,000,000 visitors saw The Harp.

THE HARP IN FRONT OF THE CONTEMPRARY ARTS BUILDING PRIOR TO BEING DESTROYED   *AUGUSTA SAVAGE*

MEMORIES

GROVER WHALEN, THE FAIR ORGANIZER, ACCEPTS A REPLICA OF THE HARP   *BLACK VISITORS TO THE FAIR*

FROM HER HANDS

"Where are you folks off to now?"

"It's time to see the Trylon and the Perisphere. Care to join along?"

"Rachel, I would be delighted. I've heard so much about them. They are most unusual constructions."

"You have the time?"

"I'll make time."

"It's hard to believe that the Fair is actually here, at this God-forsaken location."

"What are you getting at Mr. Freeman?"

"I used to drive to the train."

"I don't understand."

"Augusta, I drove a rubbish truck for the City. Flushing Meadows was where our loads were eventually dumped."

FAIR FACTS

The New York World's Fair needed a home, a location close to the city where land was inexpensive, and of little use to anyone. The organizers of the Fair finally settled on the Corona Dumps, a marshy tract that could be transformed into a 1216-acre fairground. It was an area straddling the Flushing River where New York City dumped household ash and street sweepings from Brooklyn. The ash was collected mainly by trucks and then transported by the Brooklyn Transit Company's freight trains. The trains were called the Talcum Powder Express. They were often uncovered and, given the speed of the trains and prevailing winds, a great deal of soot and ash simply flew into the surrounding hamlets along the tracks. Housewives were not happy with their newly washed clothes and sheets hanging on outdoor clotheslines. In time a mountain of ash debris rose into the sky leading to the name Corona Dumps.

A MOUNTAIN OF ASH

The land was considered worthless. Nevertheless, the City bought the land for $7,000,000 and then leased the area back to the New York World's Fair Corporation. The area was then designated the Flushing Meadows Park with the understanding that following the Fair the area would become part of the New York City park system. Reclaiming the area was quite a project. Corona Dumps was really a colossal city dump. The years of accumulated waste had to be knocked down and carted off. In total seven million cubic acres of meadow mat and refuse were moved before the land was leveled. Bogs had to be filled in. Fountain Lake had to be created. Ground breaking began on June 29, 1936. By March 1937 the renovation was completed. The job cost $12,000,000. The unwanted marshy landscape was now ready for the Fair. Thousands of architects, engineers, designers, artists, and contractors were needed to complete the job. The work would go on around the clock.

THE UNWANTED LAND

The first building erected on the future World's Fair site was a nondescript, totally unappealing structure, yet absolutely indispensable to the success of the entire project. Its name certainly didn't clamor for attention. It was called the Material Testing Building. It was used as a testing lab to make sure that all construction materials would be suitable for the marshy soil left behind from the former dump. Would the materials be able to handle the weather, especially winds and moisture? Of course, all of this raised a paradox. On the one hand the structures had to be strong to withstand the elements. On the other hand almost everything would be torn down once the Fair ended.

THE TESTING BUILDING

It is sometimes forgotten that the World's Fair Corporation was building a small city that would host millions of visitors. To do so meant a temporary administration had to be organized and housed. It takes people to run an impromptu government, even a temporary one. The necessary bureaucracy had to be housed. An Administrative Building was constructed for just that purpose. It was the first structure intended for actual use during the Fair. Though housing an army of bureaucrats the building was not without its artistic beauty.

THE NEARLY COMPLETED ADMINISTRATION BUILDING

A BEAUTIFUL BUILDING

Creating a small city is no easy task. Every pavilion needed underground electric lines, water, sewers, gas, and telephone service. That is, all the things we take for granted and cannot function without. Obviously, a large staff had to be recruited and trained, including fire and police departments. Crime and fires didn't stop at the entry to the Fair.

READY FOR ACTION

In addition to the regular police a special unit was recruited to accompany and protect special guests. The group was called the Haskell Guard. It was recruited from 19 different Indian tribes across America. The group was named after the Haskell Institute for Indians in Lawrence, Kansas and was a favorite of the president of the World's Fair, Grover Whelan.

THE HASKELL GUARD

Through excellent planning and hard work the construction of a small city was completed.

THE NEW YORK WORLD'S FAIR UNDER CONSTRUCTION

THE COMPLETED JOB

———————

"Which way to the Trylon?"

"Dad, it's in the *Guide Book*."

"So, James?"

"Just follow me. It's near the Perisphere."

CHAPTER 3 – THE FUTURE IN DESIGN

"There they are," James cried out. "Just look at them."

"I didn't realize they were so large," Martha replied with a look of astonishment in her eyes.

"They do capture one's attention."

"That they do, Mom," Rachel remarked. "I've never seen anything like them."

"That's a piece of work," Mr. Freeman said as if surveying a fine piece of machinery. "What do you think of all this, Augusta?"

Augusta Savage withheld comment for a moment as she took in the modernistic structures, what some would call monumental structures. Even as she did her hands flexed and reflexed, moving about as if molding some unseen image out of the red clay of her childhood, or the current fragile plaster of The Harp. Finally she said in a quiet but determined way, "They have a beauty, separate from each other, yet intimately connected as if they entered the world as twin siblings. They are beyond my imagination."

They gathered now as an extended family and gazed at the structures designed by Wallace Harrison and J. Andre Fouilhoux. What they were peering at was the "Theme Center" of the 1939 New York World's Fair: a whole new world on the horizon.

PERISPHERE AND TRYLON

The Perisphere was a giant sphere. It was 180 feet in diameter or about 55m for those on the metric system. The Perisphere was connected to the Trylon that rose 610-feet into the sky, spire-shaped and reminiscent of European cathedrals. It housed the longest escalator in the world. As to their names... The Trylon's name was coined from the phrase "triangular pylon." Perisphere was derived from the Greek "porefix peri" that meant all around or enclosing. The Perisphere housed a diorama by Henry Dreyfuss called "Democracity." The diorama emphasized the Fair's theme, *The World of Tomorrow*. It was depicting a utopian city of the future. Building the two structures was a challenging job. Nothing like this had ever been done before for any world's fair.

THE CONSTRUCTION PROJECT

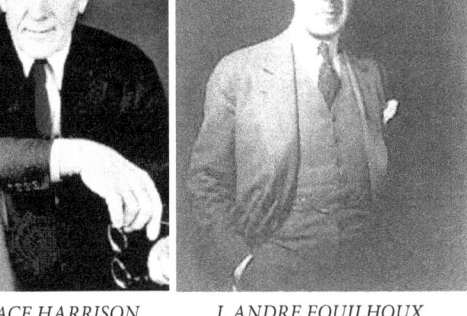

WALLACE HARRISON   J. ANDRE FOUILHOUX
DESIGNER OF THE STRUCTURES

FAIR FACTS

The Perisphere and the Trylon were constructed with 2,000 cubic yards of concrete and reinforced steel. Over 3,000 tons of structural steel rested on more than 1,000 pilings of Douglas fir creosoted for durability. The total weight of the two structures was approximately 10,000 tons.

Visitors shuffled along on a moving sidewalk within the Perisphere before taking a seat. An interior display of the utopian city was seen from above. At the same time a multi-image slide presentation was projected on the dome of the sphere. You saw the future above and below, almost simultaneously.

VIEWING CENTERTON   *BUILDING CENTERTON*

"Dad, what are people looking at once they're in the giant globe?"

"Rachel, according to the program information, the diorama features an inner city called *Centerton*. It serves as the cultural and economic hub of this perfectly planned city. Around *Centerton* are a number of satellite towns called Pleasantvilles and Millvilles. They are primarily residential with some light industry. The outer towns were separated from *Centerton* by green belts. This would provide everyone with access to parks."

"Dad, all that was in the program?"

"Yeah and a lot more."

"How did they make all those little buildings?"

"Martha, they did so carefully, accurately, and to the right ratios. No surveyor would have done better. Amazing isn't it?"

"Where do we go now?"

The family and Augusta entered the Perisphere and, along with other visitors, viewed the future community of *Centerton*. Once done they exited and headed for the Trylon. To do this they had to descend to the ground level on the third element of the Theme Center. This was the Helicline. It was a 950-foot-long spiral ramp that partially encircled the Perisphere. It was the walkway to the Trylon. This the family did along with others.

EXITING ON THE HELICLINE

"That was some stroll, Mom."

"But a beautiful one Martha. I do wonder how they came up with the word helicline."

"It's all in the guide book. The word heli comes from the Greek 'helix' that refers to a spiral incline, one that curves."

"Aren't you a font of information, my dear husband?"

"What do you think of all this, Augusta?"

Augusta glanced again at the geometric forms before her. It was almost as if she was trying to penetrate the outer coverings, seeking somehow to find the soul of the images, if not the heartbeat of their creators. In time she said to her new friends, "They are so aesthetically pleasing, complimenting each other as they do. It's difficult to believe that something so large could seem so delicate and inspiring."

————————

FAIR FACTS

The Trylon and Perisphere were the central symbol of the 1939 New York World's Fair. Their images were on post cards. Promotional materials published by the Fair Corporation focused on them. Even the US Post Office got involved.

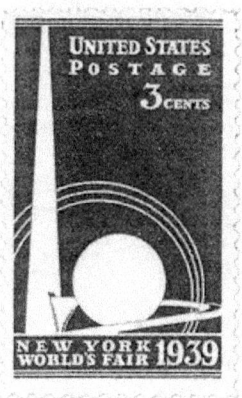

The two structures were built in Flushing Meadows Park in Queens, New York. They were intended to be temporary with steel framing and plaster board facades. Both buildings were razed and scrapped after the closing of the Fair. Their materials were not dumped into an unsightly sanitary fill, there to be covered forever with a cloak of dirt. That was not their fate. Scrap metal materials from the two structures would be used in producing armaments.

Curiously, the symbol of the later 1964-1965 New York World's Fair was the Unisphere. It was located where the Perisphere once stood. The Unisphere stood 140 feet high and was 120 feet in diameter. Over 500 steel pieces were involved in showing all the countries of the world and the great mountain ranges. Overall, the structure built by US Steel weighed over 700,000 pounds. Visitors can still see this iconic creation. New York City has maintained the structure.

THE UNISPHERE – 1964 NEW YORK WORLD'S FAIR

The Perisphere and Trylon took on a completely new appearance at night. After dusk the structures were lit up. Color filters were utilized and placed over the 5000-watt incandescent spotlights aimed at the Perisphere. Some 340 projectors and fifty-four capillary lamps banked on the roofs of nearby buildings were used for effect.

Many urban planners saw in Centerton a first vision of what was later called suburbia and a forerunner of a postwar Long Island community known as Levittown.

The twin structures were tied to the World's Fair goal that a better future awaited the world. As stated in the official pamphlet:

The eyes of the Fair are on the future---not in the sense of peering toward the unknown nor attempting to foretell the events of tomorrow and the shape of things to come, but in the sense of presenting a new and clearer view of today in preparation for tomorrow; a view of the forces and ideas that prevail as well as the machines. To its visitors the Fair will say: "Here are the materials, ideas, and forces at work in our world. These are the tools with which the World of Tomorrow must be made."

The main purpose of the Fair was to lift the spirits of America and, of course, to bring much needed business to New York City. Given the state of the country in 1939 that was a heavy lift. Millions were still out of work regardless of the New Deal's programs to improve the economy. The lingering effects of the Great Depression still haunted the great cities of the country. Abroad the world was tilting toward a war in Europe as Nazi Germany was aggressively altering the European map. In the Far East militaristic Imperial Japan was at war with China, while also coveting the oil and agricultural resources of South East Asia. The world was a tinderbox awaiting a spark. An increasing number of Americans in 1940 assumed that this might be a last summer of peace. In the meantime the Perisphere and the Trylon offered hope for a better more peaceful future.

"Why that look, Martha?"
"Mom, I was just wondering."
"Yes?"
"Centerton..."
"What about it?"
"Would we be able to live there?"

The question hung in the air, a biting reminder of how hard it was for Black families to purchase a home outside of traditional Black areas. The family had made two offers over the years to move outside of Harlem. They had not been successful. Real Estate agents and sellers were always polite, but in the end the Freemans were always turned down.

"We must hope so for your generation, Martha."
"Do you really think so, Mom?"
"I do. I must."

Augusta picked up on the painful conversation. It invoked her own efforts to purchase land for a studio outside of the city where her artistic endeavors would flourish beyond the cement and asphalt and the milling crowds of New York. She dearly wanted this Shangri-la, a place of beauty and peace, utopia for her among the wooded hills of up-state New York. She wanted what Ronald Coleman and Jane Wyatt had found in the 1937 film, *Lost Horizon.*

LOST HORIZON

Mr. Freeman interrupted Augusta's musings.

"Where should we go tomorrow?"
"Dad, let's see George and then the television exhibit."
"James, you're on a first name basis now with out first president?"

"How about GW?"

"Dear, speak to your son."

"James?"

"Okay, President George Washington."

"Good. I'd like to see this television business, too. What about you, Augusta? Can you join us?"

"I'll make some time. I will, however, miss seeing all this, what the hand of creation has brought forth."

THE CENTER OF ATTRACTION

CHAPTER 4 – THE TWO PRESIDENTS

DAY 2 – JULY 24, 1940

The Freeman family met at the Constitutional Mall. After gathering themselves following a healthy breakfast they took a local municipal bus to the railroad station outside of Harlem. There they boarded a train specifically scheduled to take visitors to the World's Fair. Reaching their destination, they used their weekly ticket to join an immense number of people entering the Fair. Many of them headed immediately toward Constitutional Mall to see the statue of George Washington by James Earl Fraser. They also came to view the "Four Freedoms," statues reflecting America's adherence to the Bill of Rights and the great liberties they enshrined.

VISITORS TO THE FAIR

THE FIRST PRESIDENT

As the family stood at the base of the statue, Mr. Freeman, *Guide Book* in hand, said, "The president is standing in his inaugural robes as he appeared 150 years ago, April 30, 1789."

"And I know where he was sworn in, Dad."

"And where was that, young man?"

"Federal Hall in our city. I think it was on Wall Street."

"It was, but that's not in the *Guide Book*. How did you know that tidbit?"

"Mr. Bechtel, my history teacher told us. And guess what?"

"What little brother?" Rachel said with a big sister look bordering on a mixture of curiosity and impatience.

"It took Washington seven days to travel from Mt. Vernon to New York. Everywhere along the line of travel he was met with adoring crowds."

"It's nice to see our tax dollars are working with James."

"Mom, he's just showing off," Martha said. "He's just trying to keep up with, Dad."

At that moment Augusta Savage arrived in her working clothes befitting a sculptor who had been working with wet clay all morning. After dusting off her hands and a quick embrace all-around she said, still a bit out of breath:

"At last I've caught up with you."

"You've been at work?"

"I have, Rachel. My hands are always busy. It is an affliction I adore, though it almost threw me off schedule today. Once I got going it was difficult to stop."

"You're working on a new project?"

"Alas, yes, Mr. Freeman."

"What do you think of the statue?" Mrs. Freeman asked.

As was her way Augusta Savage took her time before answering, at least where art was the focus.

"Fraser has done a remarkable job. That man has talent. His desire to pose Washington standing proudly on Constitutional Mall between the Trylon and the Perisphere and adjacent to the Lagoon of Nations was a stroke of genius. How inspiring! And what a sense of proportion and perspective showing our first president facing the future symbolized by an immense globe and a shaft of steel slanting into the sky. This is architecture in balance, almost poetic in the relationship of the three objects, each tied intimately to the other. I admire such work."

"Augusta, what you said is beyond my *Guide Book*."

"You must forgive me, Mr. Freeman. My creative juices sometimes get the best of me, forcing me to go on and on."

"A vice most appropriate for this Fair and much enjoyed by our family."

Interjecting himself James said, "Wouldn't it be great to be in an airplane flying above the Fair, you know, to see everything at a glance? I'd sure like to do that."

"No need for a plane, my curious, young man. The *Guide Book* has a photo you might like to see."

THE VIEW FROM ABOVE

"Aren't the Four Freedoms close by?" Rachel asked. "I hear they are something to behold."

"They're all around you," Augusta replied. "They are so inspiring in form and symbolism."

"You've seen them before?"

"Almost every day from the moment they were erected last year to this very moment. I never tire looking at them. You know each one of the statues is 31 feet tall. That's quite something. I even had a chance to see their creator, Leo Friedlander. A most interesting man."

LEO FRIEDLANDER

THE FOUR FREEDOMS ON THE CONSTITUTIONAL MALL

Speech   Press

Religion   Assembly

"Okay, my children, a simple question desiring a clear answer. What is the source of these Four Freedoms?"

"Mom, the Bill of Rights. Right?"

"Very good, James."

"Next question. Which one is most important to our people?"

"Assembly."

"Why is that, Rachel?"

"That permits us to demonstrate for our civil rights and for better opportunities. That's what you always preached to us. And isn't that what happened before the Fair opened last year when 700 Blacks protested the lack of good jobs at the Fair?"

"That is what happened."

"Did it help, Mom?"

"Very little, but it did lead to this *Negro Week* we're enjoying."

"No demonstration, no *Negro Week*?"

"Quite possibly, James."

"I'd like to make a point."

"Please," Augusta said, "What's on your mind, Mr. Freeman?"

"Assembly is important. No question about that, but so are the ideas of free speech and a free press. Together they buttress the right to assembly. Without them the word doesn't get out. That's where the Black press comes in. The white newspapers don't always cover what going on in the Black community, and when they do it's often full of stereotypes with a negative twist. It's even worse down South in Dixie where Jim Crow stuff holds reign."

"It's even here at the Fair, I'm afraid. So few Black artists were considered. I was so fortunate to get a commission. Where jobs were available for Blacks they were the lowest paid and usually the most physical. Still, some progress was made because of the demonstration mentioned earlier."

FAIR FACTS

In his 1941 State of the Union Address President Roosevelt articulated a powerful vision for a "world in which all people had freedom of speech and of religion, and freedom from want and fear." What he said came to be known as the *Four Freedoms Speech*. It was delivered on January 6, 1941. It was a light in a world consumed by the darkness of war. Much of Europe was under a brutal Nazi regime, with Germany and the Soviet Union locked in a fight to the death. In the far Pacific the war in China raged on, even as Imperial Japan prepared for an inevitable war with the United States. Before the year was out the peaceful Hawaiian waters would run red with American blood. Four years later, millions would be dead across the world. The Four Freedoms would be adopted as the foundation for a Universal Declaration of Human Rights by the United Nations in 1948.

––––––––––

"Isn't this area also where President Roosevelt opened the Fair with a speech?"

Rachel's question caught all off guard and all were happy that was so. Discussing segregation and discrimination were hardly joyous topics for a day of pleasure and amusement.

"Right over there, Rachel," said her dad.

FDR OPENS THE NEW YORK WORLD'S FAIR

––––––––––––––––––

FAIR FACTS

It was a cloudy Sunday. The date was April 30, 1939 and the New York World's Fair was having a grand opening. Some 206,000 people were in attendance. The opening date was not by accident. It coincided with the 150th anniversary of George Washington's inauguration as our first president in what we call Lower Manhattan today. Though many of the exhibits, pavilions, and other facilities were not yet ready for the opening day, President Franklin D. Roosevelt was present for the great celebration. There had been plans for the US Navy to visit New York City for the opening day following maneuvers in the Caribbean. Painful as it was for Roosevelt, being the former Secretary of the Navy under President Woodrow Wilson, those plans were cancelled. Via the Panama Canal the fleet was dispatched to the Pacific to symbolize America's resolve to counter Japan's aggressive moves in the South China Sea. The fleet would be moored at a little known location called Pearl Harbor.

As President Roosevelt spoke a television camera focused in on him. This was the first time a president would be seen on a television set and not just heard over radio. Throughout the Fair televisions were set up for visitors to see and hear the speech, mainly on 5 to 12-inch screens. In addition, about 1,000 people viewed the chief executive on about 200 television sets scattered throughout New York City.

NBC used the event to inaugurate regularly scheduled television broadcasts in the metropolitan area over their station W2XBS (called WNBC today). Of course, many people thought it was all a trick, some sort of magical manipulation of film already taken. In order to convince skeptical visitors otherwise, RCA set up one television with a transparent case so that the internal components could be seen and to show there was no film hidden inside. To further convince the disbelieving, at the RCA pavilion visitors could see themselves on television as well as watch early commercials projected by the unique technology.

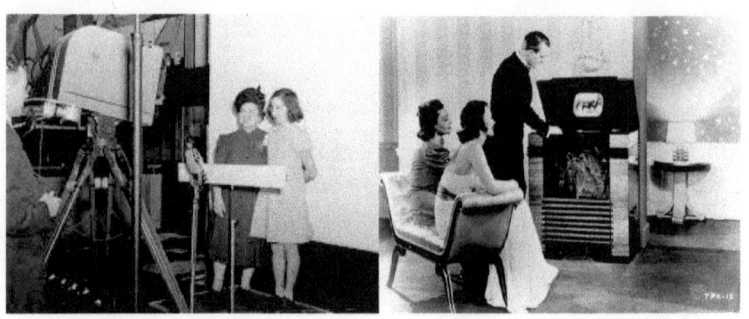

SEEING YOURSELF ON TELEVISION   *SMALL SCREEN, LARGE FURNITURE*

———————

"Dad, will we be able to buy one?"

"James, are you kidding? I would need to work ten jobs if I could get one on the installment plan. I'm afraid we'll have to get along with our old Admiral radio."

"It would be like having a movie theater in the living room."

"Possible, Martha, but can you imagine watching the *Wizard of Oz* on that small screen, or *Gone With the Wind*?"

"You do have a good point, Mom."

"What about watching the Yankees or the Dodgers? Wouldn't that be possible, Dad?"

"I guess so, James. If you can watch one thing, well why not another? What do you think, Augusta?"

As was her way Augusta Savage took a moment before answering. Again her creative nature seemed to be adding up the pluses and minuses of this new flanged creature.

"I'm not sure what my feelings are. I'm always pursued by aesthetic impulses. How does one capture the emotional intensity of the Atlanta railroad station scene portrayed in Margaret Mitchell's novel *Gone With the Wind* on a tiny screen? How do you show the awesome beauty and destructive power of the Union bombardment? How do you show Scarlett O'Hara's love of the land and the bitter fruits of her world blown away by the winds of history? Such an epic moment must be shown on a large theater screen, I think."

"People might adjust?"

"Possibly, Rachel, but what about the grand music? How would that resonate? Music, I contend, carries us forth in the film where words alone are insufficient."

"I hadn't considered that."

"Couldn't they make larger sets in time? Maybe even in color?"

"That might be the case, James."

"If I may I would like to change the topic."

"Mrs. Freeman?"

"Augusta, you were here the day President Roosevelt spoke?"

"Oh, yes. I was one of many."

"Do you recall what he said?"

————————

FAIR FACTS – THE SPEECH

From henceforth in our history the thirtieth day of April will have a dual significance: the Inauguration of the First President of the United States, which began the Executive Branch of the Federal Government, and the opening of the New York World's Fair of 1939. The United States stands today as a completely homogeneous nation, similar in its civilization from Coast to Coast and from North to South, united in a common purpose to work for the greatest good of the greatest number, united in the desire to move forward to better things in the use of its great resources of nature and its even greater resources of intelligent, educated manhood and womanhood, and united in its desire to encourage good will among nations.

All who come to this World's Fair in New York will, I need not tell them, receive the heartiest of welcomes. They will find that the eyes of the United States are fixed on the future. Yes, our wagon is still hitched to a star. It is a star of friendship, a star of progress for mankind, a star of greater happiness and less hardship, a star of international good will, and, above all, a star of peace.

PRESIDENT ROOSEVELT

"That's what I recall."

"Augusta, when the President spoke of the 'greatest good of the greatest number,' was he including Blacks?"

"I believe that was in his heart, Mrs. Freeman."

"But he hasn't undone the terrible things in the Deep South."

"Rachel, he's not a miracle worker. He can only do so much, and then only with great difficulty. I believe he cares deeply about all Americans."

"But progress is so slow."

"That's why we keep fighting, children."

"Dad, what do you think?"

"Martha, nothing comes easy for us. We're in a constant struggle to ensure our rights under the Constitution. Emancipation set us free. It didn't guarantee full equality with others. That's up to us to achieve. Do you agree, Augusta?"

"An image please... When I look at a slab of marble I must envision a face not yet visible but inherently present if only I can chip away here and there to uncover what was always there. That's the way I see the President's speech. We must continue to chip away at the marble. More of what we seek is revealed each day."

"It seems like it's a large chunk of marble."

"James, you do have a way with words, but you're right and so what? Our choice is to give up in dismay and frustration or to sally forth undeterred by bumps in the road."

"Lots of bumps."

THE STRUGGLE

The little gathering quieted. What had been said required no additional talk. As always it was time to move on.

"Dad, what's next?"

"Rachel, first lunch and then we head to the time capsule."

CHAPTER 5 – THE TIME CAPSULE

THAT AFTERNOON

The Freeman family was grouped together in what appeared to be a large storage center. Others were with them, all restricted to one section by a colorful yellow rope tied securely to large, upright metallic canisters. They were listening to a cheerful, somewhat roundish person who could have played center on a football team before becoming an anthropologist at Syracuse University. After some routine introductions and the placement of diagrams, pictures, and objects, he got down to business.

"I'm Professor Art Miller. I'm your host for the next thirty minutes. I'm here to explain what took place here on September 23, 1938, the precise moment of the Autumnal Equinox. That was when a Time Capsule was buried beneath your feet. As determined by the U.S. National Geodetic Survey the exact location was 40 degrees 44' 34.09" N and 73 degrees 50' 43.84" W. The capsule was buried fifty feet in the ground. It cannot be opened until the 7th millennium or the year 6900 by the people of that day. If present day ways of determining time are non-existent future generations can determine the age of the Time Capsule by using astronomical data. On May 3rd of this year there was an eclipse of the moon. There will be another one on October 8, 1939. Using the astronomical data provided future folks will be able to determine the age of the capsule and when it was buried. A record book about this capsule has been given to thousands of libraries, museums, and depositories worldwide to preserve the knowledge of its existence. And that information includes where the capsule is located. The diagrams before you illustrate the Time Capsule."

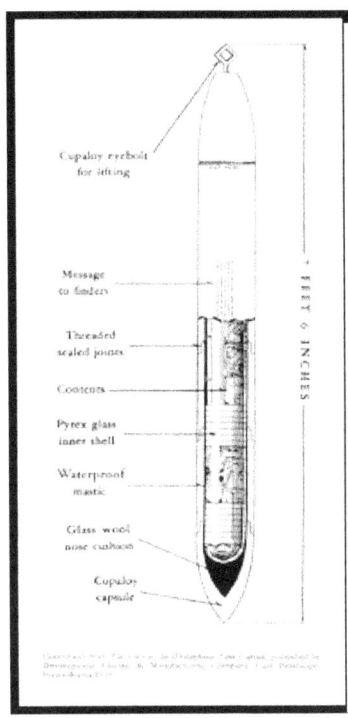
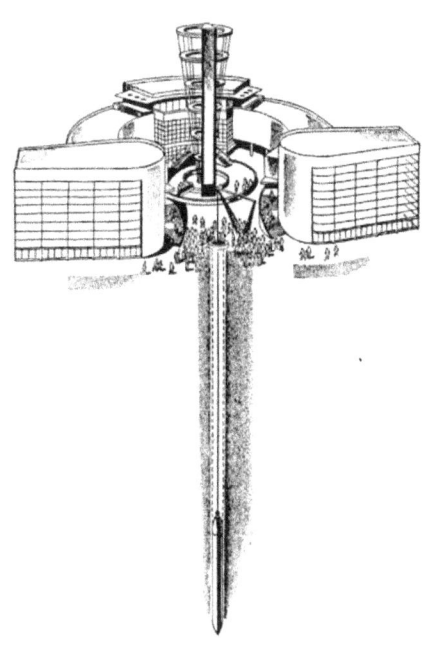

"You should know that the Westinghouse Electric and Manufacturing Company prepared the capsule. As you will note the time capsule is bullet-shaped. It measures seven and a half feet in length and is 8.75 inches in diameter. It is buried 50 feet deep in marshy soil. It is covered with pitch and concrete. It is made of a non-ferrous alloy called Cupaloy. This is a new alloy created especially for this project. In theory it is designed to resist corrosion for 5,000 years. If it doesn't someone in the future can sue Westinghouse. For those interested in technical information this new alloy is composed of 99.4% copper, 0.5% chromium, and 0.1% silver. It has the strength of steel."

"Let me stop for a minute. Are there any questions?" Before anyone could speak James Freeman shouted out in his youthful enthusiasm, "What's in the time capsule?"

"That is the question, young man. I will elucidate."

_____

- one fountain pen.
- an alphabet block set.
- over 70 types of fabrics, metals, and plastics.
- micro files recording our contemporary art and news events.
- micro files containing over 10,000,000 words and 1,000 pictures.
- a microfilm viewer is included along with a motion picture projector for viewing newsreels.
- a Sears Roebuck catalog.
- a dictionary and an almanac.
- a pack of Camel cigarettes.
- a variety of seeds were placed in sealed glass vials (corn, wheat, cotton, flax, tobacco, rice, soy beans, carrots, barley, and sugar beets).

"The contents of the capsule were recorded in a *Book of Record of the Time Capsule of Cupaloy*. Hopefully this record will assist people in the year 6939 in locating and recovering the capsule. The following photograph displayed on the screen before you showed the actual event when the capsule was buried."

LOWERING THE TIME CAPSULE

FAIR FACTS

In 1964, New York held another World's Fair. Once more a Time Capsule was buried. It was referred to as Time Capsule II. It rests ten feet north of the first capsule. At the close of the World's Fair in 1965 it was decided to construct a permanent sentinel to indicate the location of both capsules. The Rock of Ages Corporation built a seven-ton granite monument for this purpose.

THE TIME CAPSULES
DEPOSITED
SEPTEMBER 23, 1938
AND
OCTOBER 16, 1965
BY THE
WESTINGHOUSE ELECTRIC CORPORATION
AS A RECORD OF
TWENTIETH CENTURY CIVILIZATION
TO ENDURE FOR 5,000 YEARS

"Are there any additional questions?"

"I understand there are letters enclosed in the capsule," Rachel Freeman blurted out. "Is that true?"

"In Time Capsule I, yes. Three in fact: one each from Albert Einstein, Robert Andrews Millikan, and Thomas Mann. Copies of their letters are available in the Fair Book Store. I will, however, paraphrase the letters for you."

Albert Einstein

"The eminent mathematician spoke of the present and future with hope and fear. Given our present world situation we should reflect on what he said."

Our time is rich in inventive minds, the inventions of which could facilitate our lives considerably. However, the production and distribution of commodities is entirely unorganized so that everybody must live in fear of being eliminated from the economic cycle, in this way suffering for the want of everything. Furthermore, people living in different countries kill each other at irregular intervals, so that also for this reason any one who thinks about the future must live in fear and terror.

ALBERT EINSTEIN

Robert Andrews Millikan

"This experimental physicist also warned of the possibilities facing humanity. His message was clear."

At this moment, August 22, 1938, the principles of representative ballot government, such as are represented by the governments of the Anglo-Saxon, French, and Scandinavian countries, are in a deadly conflict with the principles of deposition, which up to two centuries ago had controlled the destiny of man throughout practically the whole of recorded history. If the rational, scientific, progressive principles win out in this struggle, there is the possibility of a warless, golden age ahead. If the reactionary principles of despotism triumph now and in the future, the future of mankind will repeat the sad story of war and oppression as in the past.

ROBERT MILLIKAN

Thomas Mann

"This German novelist and social critic also cried out for a future of peace and rational harmony. With Europe on the verge of war his words ring with consequence for all of us."

We know that the idea of the future as a "better world" was a fallacy of the doctrine of progress. The hopes we center on you, citizens of the future, are in no way exaggerated. In broad outline, you will actually resemble us very much as we resemble those who lived a thousand or five thousand years ago. The optimistic conception of the future is a projection into time of an endeavor, which does not belong to the temporal world... This is an endeavor on the part of man to approximate to his idea of himself, the humanization of man. Brothers of the future unite with us in this endeavor.

THOMAS MANN

_____

"I see our time is up. I trust I have been somewhat helpful in explaining the nature and importance of our Time Capsule. Please exit through the doors on your left."

Outside the Freeman family gathered themselves before moving on to the next item on their agenda. But first a few things needed to be discussed. Mrs. Freeman got the ball rolling.

"Did those letters seem optimistic to you? I'm just not sure."

"Mom, Einstein, I think, shuddered at our prospects to avoid another world war. That's what I got out of it, you know, talking about living in 'terror and fear.'"

"Rachel, I picked up on that too," Martha added. "I think he was losing hope about chances to survive another terrible war, or even a worse one after that."

"All I know is that countries everywhere are arming to the teeth in preparation for something. Roosevelt is pouring tons of money into rearmament."

"All too true," Rachel quickly responded to her father.

"What's your take, James?" Mrs. Freeman asked.

"If you really want to know?"

"We do."

"Well, two things. First, another war would probably foul up getting a basketball scholarship."

"Because?"

"Because, Rachel, the draft would probably recruit me before a basketball coach."

It dawned on all that the family was not immune from the hypothetical. If war broke out James would be drafted. He was big, strong, and healthy, a perfect specimen for the military. This realization brought a noticeable shudder to Mrs. Freeman. Her husband picked up on that, saying, "We'll cross that bridge when we have to."

"The Millikan letter seemed to support Einstein. A war looms between democracy and dictatorships. That's the way I see it. My teacher calls Nazi Germany and Soviet Russia totalitarian states, oppressive and militaristic. He thinks a war is coming."

"Hard to deny that, James," Mr. Freeman said. "Hard to deny that."

"Not another war…Not another member of the Freeman family dying in some foreign land."

"Mom, your Uncle Harry died bravely and with honor in France in 1918."

"Only two weeks before the Armistice was signed to end the insanity of all that business."

"Mom…"

"Rachel, the War Department sent us that terrible message. '*We regret to inform you…*' As to honors that came afterwards in the Black press… Hardly a mention in the white papers about all the boys from Harlem who never came home."

"And those who did come home weren't permitted to march in the victory parade with white soldiers," Mr. Freeman said gravely. "Our boys had to have their own parade down 5th Avenue and into Harlem. One hell of a deal."

GOING TO FRANCE   THE BIG PARADE IN HARLEM

Around the little family others went about their business viewing the exhibits and taking in the sights and sounds of the Fair. Had they listened in on the Freeman family they would have heard...

"I need to get something off my chest."

"Martha?"

"Mom, they never mentioned us."

"What are you talking about?"

"Mom, what's going into the Time Capsule, well, it's all about white people. I don't think Blacks were included. Am I wrong?"

"No, sadly you're right. There was no mention of Black music and literature, our songs and poetry."

"Nor was there any inclusion of our history, first as slaves and then as second class citizens still punished by racists attitudes. It's like we've been completely written out of history."

"Martha, what you say cannot be denied if this is indeed the case."

"They could at least include jazz and the music of our churches."

"Dad, right on."

"James, your thoughts?"

"Aren't we already excluded from professional football and baseball? Isn't it a white man's game that I have no hope of breaking into because of my color? I'm forced to play in the Negro Leagues, if I play at all in professional sports."

"Don't knock those guys. They're as good as the white players. Josh Gibson was as good as Babe Ruth."

"I didn't mean any disrespect, Dad."

"I know that."

"Josh Gibson?"

"Rachel, a few facts. Josh Gibson was known as the 'Black Babe Ruth.' During his long career with the Washington Homestead Grays, one of the first professional Negro League teams, he slugged some 800 home runs, many of them tape-measured blasts. In 1936 he reportedly hit 84 over the wall. He led the league for ten consecutive years as a hitter. His career batting average was .347. In the few opportunities he had to bat against white major league stars in exhibition games he had a .426 batting average. If the gods of baseball are fair in the future maybe he'll be inducted into the Baseball Hall of Fame. That would be nice. The same goes for old rubber arm."

"Who, Dad?"

"Rachel, Satchel Paige is perhaps the greatest living Black pitcher in professional baseball. Given the opportunity he always pitched well against his white counterparts. Still, no team was willing to break the ban, even if his talents would help them to win. Ironic, isn't it? Along with a lot of other talented guys he is forced to play in the Negro Leagues where only the Black press covered their exploits. Damn shame."

"That's why we root for the New York Bombers, isn't it?"

"The Yankees are great. The Dodgers play with heart and the Giants challenge each year, but no Black is on any of these teams. Our boys play for the Bombers, the "Black Yankees" of the city."

THE BLACK BABE RUTH   *SATCHEL PAIGE*

Inexplicably, Mr. Freeman's voice changed from seriousness to lightheartedness. Of course, James picked up on this immediately, asking, "What's happening, Dad?"

"I just remembered an amusing anecdote alluding to Gibson's prodigious talents."

"Which you will share, dear husband."

"It was about a homerun he hit in Pittsburgh. As the story goes …Gibson swung and the ball leaped out of the ballpark like it had been shot from a cannon. It cleared the fence and sailed out of sight. During the next day the ball came down in Philadelphia and landed in the outfielder's glove. The on-the-spot umpire looked at Gibson and then yelled for the world to hear, 'You're out yesterday in Pittsburgh!'"

"Was he as good as Ruth, Dad?"

"Certainly his equal. Beyond that, well we'll never know, but I think so."

A brisk wind kicked up, a gift of the New York Sound. Visitors feeling the cold grasp hurried to indoor venues, even as men pulled their fedoras down more securely, and women followed in suit to keep their hats from sailing away to Long Island. The chilling wind suggested a storm was brewing. It was time to get undercover.

"Let's head for the *Hot Mikado*."

"Augusta said she would meet us there. Right, Mom?"

"That's the plan. She also wants us to meet someone special."

"Who?"

"Rachel, it's a surprise."

————————

FAIR FACTS

In 1940, a British artist and novelist traveling in the United States decided to take in the New York World's Fair. His name was Percy Wyndham Lewis. He was immediately struck by the contradictions inherent in the Fair's efforts to strike a balance between the hopes of the nation and the deteriorating world situation. In 1939, the Fair's theme was hopeful: *A World of Tomorrow*. By 1940 the theme recognized a new reality: *Peace and Freedom*. The maelstrom of armed conflict inundating the world had come to New York. Lewis would return to England but not before leaving his observations.

A World's Fair and a World War, in the same compartment of time, somehow do not harmonize. A visit to the former, with one's mind numbed by the latter, makes one a bad Fairgoer. A conflict is set up; one sees more, and one sees less, of the Fair than otherwise one would. Gazing at the massed fountains, you think of the flamethrowers. Looking at death's head of the Peruvian mummy, you recall the unburied, helmeted dead of the battlefield. As you make your way down the "Court of Peace," you balk at the nomenclature, instead of, as you should, appreciating the good intentions.

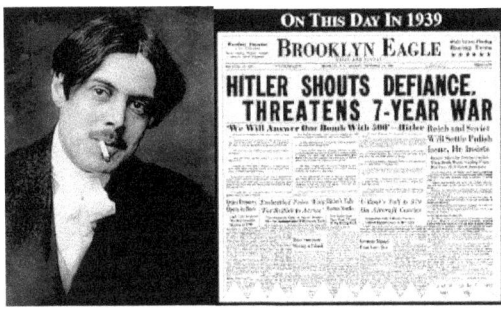

THE WAR CRITIC   AT THE ABYSS 1939

FAIR FACTS

The New York World's Fair was conceived during the Great Depression when millions were out of work and far too many families were desperate for a hot meal, a roof over their head, and clothes for their children. Though the New Deal programs implemented by the FDR Administration had provided temporary relief and cautious hope for better times, the faltering economy had not yet ignited ongoing prosperity. As envisioned by the Fair Committee a world's fair in New York City would offer a fantastic view of the future and perhaps lift millions out of the doldrums of hard times. To accomplish this the planners wanted the world's fair to be an international event by inviting the world's nations to participate. Reaching this goal would be possible by dividing the Fair into zones, each focusing on a different aspect of life. This division of emphasis provided visitors with options as to where they would spend their time.

The Government Zone

This zone was located on the eastern bank of the Flushing River. Visitors to this zone could learn about the history and culture of 60 participating countries by visiting any of the 21 pavilions. Pulling all of this together was a central Court of Peace and a Lagoon of Nations. In addition many states had their own exhibits that showcased the diversity of America.

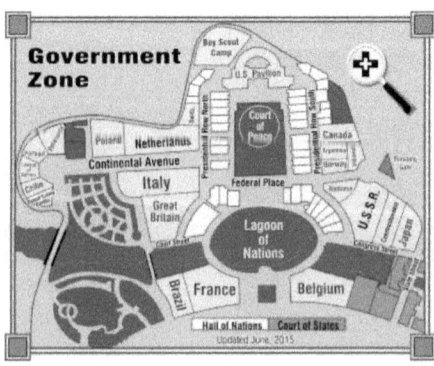

The British Pavilion, by way of example, contained a copy of the Magna Carta, the famous document ushering in rudimentary rights of nobles to control their kings beginning with King John on June 15, 1215. Some would argue that this document was the source of our own Constitution and Bill of Rights. Because Britain went to war against Germany in August 1940 the precious document was housed in Fort Knox until peace was restored in late 1945.

Yasuo Matsui, a Japanese-American architect, designed the Japanese Pavilion to resemble a traditional Shinto shrine, set within a Japanese garden. It provided a tea ceremony and Japanese flower arrangement exhibits. The interior of the shrine had a "Diplomat Room" that featured a Liberty Bell made out of Japanese pearls and diamonds, worth $1 million. One wonders what Paul Revere would have thought about that?

JAPANESE PAVILION

The American Pavilion was called the United States Federal Building. It contained 23 exhibits representing 22 states and Puerto Rico. The world's largest carillon was installed in the spire of the Florida state exhibition building. It consisted of 75 tubular bells and weighed 25 tons. The Stephen Foster Memorial Association of Florida donated the instrument.

UNITED STATES FEDERAL BUILDING

The Jewish Palestine Pavilion was unique in that no Jewish State existed at the time. What existed was the vision of a future Israel. The center of the pavilion was a monumental hammered copper relief sculpture on the façade entitled *The Scholar, The Laborer, and the Tiller of the Soil*. It was produced by Maurice Ascalon, an Art Deco sculptor. The pavilion opened on May 28, 1939 one day after Cuba denied entry of Jewish immigrants fleeing Nazi Germany aboard the *MS St. Louis*.

THE JEWISH PALESTINE PAVILION

The Scholar, The Laborer,
and the Tiller of the Soil

One structure in the Government Zone conjured up mixed emotions, both hope and despair. Hope that a European conflict might be avoided. Despair that nations were again at the abyss. It was a circular turret that symbolized unity. It was on top of a pentagonal designed base representing the five races of mankind. It portrayed the advancements in the fields of economics, health, communications, and medications. It also advanced the idea of disarmament and the peaceful resolution of conflicts. The structure was called the League of Nations.

THE LEAGUE OF NATIONS

The Food Zone

This zone showcased the industries and companies that helped make and distribute food to the nation's consumers. Major American companies participated. They, of course, featured their products. It was great advertising as they made their products available to visitors to the World's Fair. The companies involved included: Borden Dairy Company, General Cigar, Heinz, Swift, Beach Nut, Wonder Bread, and many others. The Food Zone also included restaurants where a good meal could be had in addition to the equivalent of today's fast food spots for the visitor on a tighter budget.

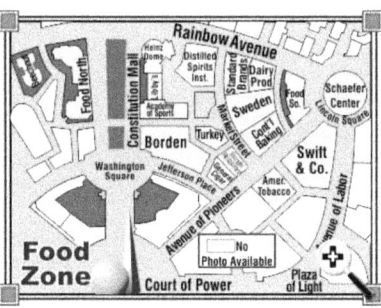

THE BORDEN (DAIRY) PAVILION

ELISE THE COW
BORDON COMPANY MASCOT

THE HEINZ DOME
57 VARIETIES OF FOOD PRODUCTS

SWIFT MEATPACKING COMPANY

The Communication and Business Zone

Fairgoers walking along the Avenue of Patriots soon encountered the Communication and Business Zone. This zone showcased a variety of companies with their state-of-the-art products and services. The companies included: Radio Corporation of America (RCA), the American Telephone and Telegraph Company (AT&T), Crosley Electronic Company, the International Business Corporation (IBM), and Aetna Life Insurance Company. The focal point of the zone was the Communications Building. This was a large structure with a pair of 160-foot high pylons flanking it.

THE COMMUNICATIONS BUILDING

In the AT&T exhibit there was a mechanized, synthetic voice that spoke to the visitors. The device simulated the human voice. It was called Voder. It anticipated the use of electronic voice machines. On the outside of the building were two murals on the façade in glass mosaic. One was called *Communication of Thought by Sound and the Spoken World*. The other mural was called *Communication of Thought by Sight and the Written World*.

AMERICAN TELEPHONE AND TELEGRAPH PAVILION

In the IBM pavilion there was a display of electric typewriters and an "electric" calculator that used punch cards. The National Cash Register Company had one of the most interesting pavilions to house its exhibits. This was also true of the Westinghouse Hall of Power where visitors ascended the pavilion by way of an electric stairway.

The Transportation Zone

Of course the Transportation Zone was about transportation. The major automobile companies had exhibits. They included: Ford, General Motors, and Chrysler. Even the tire companies got into the show with the Firestone exhibition. The zone also included advances in railroads, aviation, and marine transportation.

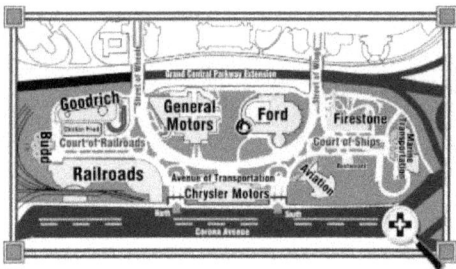 

THE FORD PAVILION

The General Motors Pavilion had an exhibit called Futurama. It presented a possible model of the transportation world some 20 years in the future. The Futurama was characterized by a series of automated highways and sprawling suburbs across the country. It introduced the public to the notion of a network of expressways connecting the nation across mountains, over rivers and lakes, through cities and towns, and never deviating from a direct course. It was hoped this vision would eventually lead to an "interstate highway program" that would connect and unite the country. Such a system would emphasize safety, comfort, speed, and economy.

The Transportation Zone also included the newest streamline railroad engines and a trackless train that ran on rubber tires.

RAIL TRANSPORTATION   TRACKLESS TRAIN

Advanced technology was prominent in the World's Fair. This was especially true of Elektro the Robot, which was constructed by the Westinghouse Electric Corporation in 1937-1938. Elektro stood seven feet tall and weighted 265 pounds. The robot was humanoid in appearance. By voice command it could walk, and move its head and arms. It could speak approximately 700 words. With charm it could smoke a cigarette or blow up balloons. Elektro's body consisted of a steel gear, cam and motor skeleton covered by an aluminum skin. The eyes were photoelectric, meaning it could distinguish between red and green light. To keep the Elektro from getting lonely Sparko was built in 1939. This was a robot dog that could bark, sit, and get to humans. The two were a big hit. Science fiction writers, it is assumed, were struck by the myriad of potential plot lines.

ELEKTRO AND SPARKO

The Amusement Zone

Located south of the World's Fair Boulevard on the eastern shore of Fountain Lake were 230 acres set aside for fun and entertainment. It was known as the Amusement Zone or simply as the Amusement Area. Without question, it was the most popular attraction in 1939-1940. People came to the New York World's Fair for many reasons. Some came to see and tour the international pavilions and perhaps consider a later trip to some far away location. Some came to see the latest products and inventions, and the technologies of the future.

Others came to experience a menagerie of animals from around the world, as well as circus-type performers such as jugglers and acrobats. Thousands enjoyed the rides including toboggans, roller coasters, and spaceships. Two particular rides were of interest to many visitors: the bobsled and a parachute tower promoted by the makers of Life Savers. Less exciting was a ride for children and their less risky parents. It was a 3' narrow gauge train ride called the Gimbels Flyer. In short, there was something for everyone.

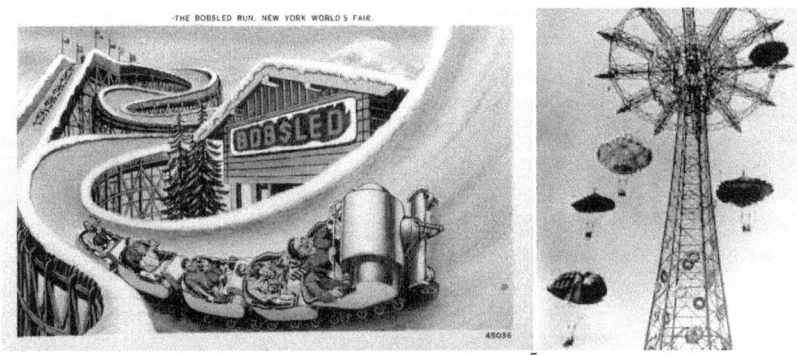

THRILL RIDES

A QUIETER THRILL

The Amusement Zone had an endless number of places to dine with meals for every possible budget. There were also games of chance with plenty of prizes. Critics of the Zone thought the area too "tacky, loud, and garish." They were, of course, outnumbered by the huge throngs who enjoyed themselves while overlooking these problematic shortcomings. Though the Fair focused on the future it still remained connected to the present. There were a number of shows that featured scantily clad, very lovely women revealing to the world the oldest of attractions. Visitors were not put off by what some called "low minded entertainment."

GIRLIE SHOWS

AMUSEMENT ZONE VISITORS

The planners of the New York World's Fair spent $250,000 to build the Music Hall in the Amusement Zone. The architects of Radio City Music Hall created an "acoustical and comfort" wonder that seated 2,375 people and had a stage that was sixty-five feet wide and fifty-six feet deep. Performances were excellent but attendance was skimpy given the $2.50 price for a ticket. Something had to be done. It was decided to alter the stage somewhat. Scenery was built on platforms to facilitate rapid changes. All that was needed was a show that would lure customers.

World's Fair Music Hall

New York World's Fair 1939

THE MUSIC HALL

It was in the Amusement Zone that Augusta Savage and the Freeman family met outside of the Music Hall on their way to see Bill Robinson in the *Hot Mikado*.

"Dad, where's Augusta? She said she'd meet us by the Music Hall."

"James, look over to your left. There she is."

Indeed, Augusta Savage was there talking to two men, each of whom seemed absorbed in showing her what turned out to be sheet music. Unlike earlier in the day when she wore her work clothes, she now had on a lively, multi-colored dress and a charming hat to ward off the sun once it peeked through the overcast. As the Freeman family approached she waved them over to her, even as a large group of visitors gathered in front of the Music Hall in preparation to enter the venue. As they neared James blurted out, "Augusta, you look different." With a charming smile she answered, "Well, thank you, James. I trust that was a compliment? You know even an artist needs to take a break from dusty, old plaster." Somewhat caught off guard by this James said a little shyly, "You look great."

Augusta quickly introduced the family to her two friends. One, as it turned out, was William Grant Still and the other was W.C. Handy. Introductions were made all around.

"W.C. Handy, oh I love your music, Sir. I especially liked *The Saint Louis Blues*. The music just got to me."

"Madam, I'm glad to hear it."

"And I loved *Memphis Blues*," Rachel intoned above the din of others. "I just wanted to get up and dance."

"And what about *Beale Street Blues*," Martha said. "That was a catchy tune."

"Well, Augusta, I must say it's a delight to meet your friends. They are gracious critics."

Augusta turned to the family to introduce the other gentleman. "I'd like you to meet the man who wrote the theme music for the Fair. This is William Grant Still."

WILLIAM GRANT STILL

———————————

FAIR FACTS

The New York World's Fair Committee had a problem in 1937 as it planned for the opening date next year. Every world's fair needed a musical theme, something that caught the visitor's senses and would years later be a joyous reminder of a day long ago. The problem, of course, was how to choose a score in the most neutral way. The decision was made to have a color-blind competition. Compositions would be submitted without any attached name or photograph. As was expected a great many submissions inundated the Fair Committee.

In the end, two theme songs were taken under consideration: *Lenox Avenue* and *A Deserted Plantation*. The Fair Committee was shocked to discover that both songs were written by the same person --- William Grant Still. This was when the color-blind competition ran into considerable push back. Still was a Black man. The issue of race challenged the Committee's choice. To the Committee's credit, however, it stuck to its guns. Still got the commission. In time he wrote *Rising Tide* (sometimes referred to as *Victory Tide*).

The *New York Age* (a Black newspaper) covered the selection process and final choice, stating: "Do you know that the theme song of the New York World's Fair was written by a Black boy? If there is an art in which this race excels, it is music."

Rising Tide would be played on a constant 6-minute loop inside the Perisphere for the exhibit Democracity (the City of Tomorrow). Andre Kostelanetz conducted the recording of Still's orchestration.

Still and Handy were joined at the hip in developing music for the Fair. In this famous photo they consult in front of the Trylon and the Perisphere, which were still under construction. The date is July 28, 1938.

During his lifetime William Grant Still composed nearly 200 works, including five symphonies, four ballets, nine operas, and over thirty choral works. He was the first Black American to conduct a major symphony orchestra (the Los Angeles Philharmonic in 1936). Still has aptly been called the "Dean of Afro-American Composers."

————————

After some chit-chat it was time to enter the Music Hall. Looking around the gathering throng of visitors, Mrs. Freeman was dismayed. How could they possibly get a good seat, she thought? This she explained to Augusta.

"Mrs. Freeman, not to worry. Thanks to Mr. Still your family has reserved seats in the second row, up front. You'll probably feel like you're on stage."

"I'm not sure if we can afford those seats."

"You are special guests of the Fair Committee. There is no charge."

"Mr. Still, my eternal thanks."

"No need. Augusta has told me about your family. It was my pleasure to assist. Do enjoy the show. The *Hot Mikado* is pure entertainment. Now follow me. We'll enter through a side door."

The family followed their new acquaintances. They were soon seated. The musical would begin in about twenty minutes. It was at this point that James made a confession in a rasped voice. "Mom, I have no idea what this show is all about."

Responding quickly, Rachel said somewhat curtly, "It's a love story written by two Englishmen that takes place in Japan, and is performed today by an all-Black cast led by Bill "Bojangles" Robinson, who was considered the best "hoffer" in town."

"Hoffer?"

"Dancer."

"Thanks, that clears up everything."

BILL "BOJANGLES" ROBINSON IN THE HOT MIKADO

"Rachel, take mercy on your little brother. You know the show frontwards and backwards."

"Okay, Dad, but James is no longer a little brother. He towers over me and Martha."

"Nevertheless."

"James, the *Hot Mikado* is a musical adaptation of Gilbert and Sullivan's 1885 comic operetta."

"Who?"

GILBERT AND SULLIVAN

"Gilbert and Sullivan."

"Who?"

"Dad, James is sounding like an owl."

"Tell him, Rachel."

"They lived during the Victorian period in England. W.S. Gilbert was the dramatist. Arthur Sullivan was the composer. Between 1871 and 1896 they jointly produced fourteen comic operas, including, *H.M.S. Pinafore*, *Pirates of Penzance*, and *The Mikado*. The British public loved their "topsy-turvy" world of fantasy and absurdity. They were also a big hit in our country. Does that help, James?"

"Okay, I've got the G and S bit, but what about the play. Mom tried to explain it to me."

"I did but with little success. Martha, why don't you take a stab at it."

"The setting is Imperial Japan, not England, and certainly not New York City. As to the story line… Nanki-Poo is a wandering minstrel in disguise. He falls in love with Yum-Yum and wants to marry her. Got that?"

James nodded, puzzlement still on his face.

"But there's a problem. Nanki-Poo is supposed to marry Katisha, an elderly lady. To avoid this he escapes and goes to Titpu. Now Nanki-Poo is really the son of the Mikado of Japan, who is like our President or a British king. Got the hang of it?"

"Sort of."

"Go on, Martha."

"Right, Dad. Yum-Yum is the ward of Ko-Ko, who is the High Executioner of Titpu. She is betrothed to him. Of course, she'd really like to get out of that marriage. Into this situation comes the Mikado. That really complicates things."

"What happens then?"

"What do you think, dear brother?"

"Yum-Yum and Nanki-Poo elope to a strange island where no one can find them. Right?"

"Wrong."

"Well, what happened?"

"I'm not telling. You'll just need to see the show."

With that the Freeman family followed Augusta and her friends into the Music Hall to see the hottest show outside of Broadway. They also saw some of the wildest, craziest costumes ever worn on the stage.

LEFT TO RIGHT: ROSETTA LE NOIRE AS PEEP-BO, MAURICE ELLIS AS POO-BAH.
FREDDIE ROBINSON AS THE MESSAGER BOY, BILL ROBINSON AS THE MIKADO,
AND ROSA BROWN AS KATISHA.

DANCING UP A STORM

FAIR FACTS

The New York World's Fair Committee constantly denied any bias in its hiring practices. This statement was made numerous times. Be that as it may Blacks filled only three significant positions in the Fair. Two of these people we already know: William Grant Still and Augusta Savage. The third person was Walter L. Roberts. He was hired as a draftsman. More typically, Blacks were employed as entertainers, often in roles that fit common stereotypes and assumptions about race in America in 1939. This was even true of the *Hot Mikado*.

In 1939 *The Crisis* spoke out against the exclusion of jobs for Blacks, except in the "capacities of maids and porters." The paper --- catering to the Harlem community ---called upon the Fair to champion "justice of opportunity." The Harlem Community Cultural Conference stated in May 1939, "the Negro is being given only a menial part in a great fair which is supposed to typify the truly democratic "world of tomorrow."

"That was some show, Dad."

"James, it's nice to know that Gilbert and Sullivan have won you over."

"I think it was Yum-Yum that did it. She was so beautiful."

"Uh-oh, I think your son has been smitten by more than an English stage play."

"Augusta, that seems to be the case," Martha said with a knowing smile.

The Freeman family was standing with Augusta Savage outside of the Hall of Music. Both William Grant Still and W.C. Handy, having said their goodbyes, were off to a project in need of their talents. Around them were others who had seen the *Hot Mikado* and were chatting about it. One common refrain was the wild costuming, especially Rosa

Brown's outfit, a winged dress with a train and a gigantic hat, weighing thirty-five pounds. Some mentioned the jazzed-up score and the sheer spectacle of the play. Almost all agreed with the critics who hailed the show as having a "full-voiced, star-studded cast to back up its sass." They also proclaimed the adaptation "as the best all-around musical show" of the year. Without question, the musical score combining riveting jazz, the Blues, hot Gospel singing, and rock won the day, as it would for two seasons of the New York World's Fair. Not to be forgotten was that the popular attraction employed an all-Black cast of 150 actors.

Martha and Rachel, always lovely, now radiated with blissful smiles. Asked about that Rachel said, "It was wonderful to see Black performers, singing, dancing, and bringing joy and pride to our people and others."

"I agree," Martha joined in. "The all-Black cast was just terrific."

"And for once, racial prejudice seemed to take a big backseat," Mr. Freeman found himself saying.

FAIR FACTS

Before the Urban League in New York City, Grover Whalen, the Fair's President, said before the Fair opened:

Wherever we who are running the Fair, where there are outstanding contributions made by your race, I assure you that they will be recognized.

In another speech he said:

The World of Tomorrow on view at the Fair would be achieved when everyone utilized cooperation to preserve and save the best of our modern civilization.

On another occasion he remarked:

This is your Fair, built for you and dedicated to you. You will find it a never ceasing source of wonder.

Speaking as the President of the Fair Committee, Grover Whalen spoke to the theme of the New York World's Fair:

This great exposition is an achievement so timely as to be of transcendental significance. Architecture, the arts, science, finance, government, education and religions...all have given of their best talent in order to prove the truth of the premise (that we are on the threshold of a new era of greater promise). Time alone can reveal the ultimate effect of this colossal achievement.

Countering Whalen's idealistic statements was a resolution passed by the NAACP:

In an exposition that purports to indicate the trend toward the world of tomorrow, this association believes that among the first considerations should have been a recognition of the unfairness of discrimination between people and the justice of opportunity for all on the basis of merit. We condemn the restrictions on employment at the New York World's Fair based on race and color.

There was no official policy of racial discrimination. There was, however, an apparent lack of Black participation, perhaps the inevitable outcome of racial attitudes of the day.

"Where do we go tomorrow?" James asked, already knowing what he wanted to see.

"We ladies are going to Rose McClendon Players, where they are performing a sketch about Booker T. Washington," Mrs. Freeman said.

"And then we're going to see the Karamu Dancers of Cleveland, Ohio," Martha added.

"After that, if there's time, we want to hear Eubie Blake, the jazz trumpeter," Rachel pointed out to all.

"So, Dad, where are you and James headed?"

"Martha, we're headed to more civilized horizons. Tell them, James."

"We have a date with Clark Kent and Frank Buck."

CHAPTER 8 – AUGUSTA

DAY 3 – JULY 25, 1940

The Freeman ladies met Augusta Savage at the Louisiana Beef BBQ. After surveying the lunch menu overly generous helpings of tender tasting beef flavored with a sauce known only to the proprietor were ordered. The beef came with corncobs, crisply cooked over an outdoor fire pit, and garnished with butter and another seasoning that tempted and delighted. More than a spoonful of baked beans also graced their plates. Large glasses of cool lemonade completed their meal.

"My gracious, I'll never be able to devour this plate," Mrs. Freeman said as she lightly took a bite of the beef,

"Unlike some places in the Food Court this place certainly didn't skimp on the portions," Martha said in response to her mother's somewhat plaintive words.

"And the price seems so reasonable," Rachel added. "Dad would have loved this place."

"Where are your father and James?"

"Augusta, they're off to see Superman."

"Rachel, I had forgotten. Today is *Superman Day* at the Fair."

"No way my husband could say no to James. The kid is making money for *D.C. Comics* all by himself."

At that moment a brawny, yet charming Black man came to their table. He wore a splattered apron, suggesting that he had been hard at work preparing food for his patrons. Bearing a big smile he said, "Augusta, is everything okay, the food and drinks?"

"Ralph, just fine and my hearty thanks."

"Wonderful. If you wish for second helpings, just wave."

Augusta simply nodded and Ralph departed to his fire pits.

"Augusta, is there something you would like to tell us?"

"Mrs. Freeman, a confession. I have known Ralph since the Fair opened last year. At times we were the only two Blacks in our area of the Fair. We learned we were both from Florida, as was his wife who does the business part of their enterprise in addition to baking great desserts. We quickly became close friends and barter partners. I gave their ten-year-old girl lessons in sculpting and he provided a needed meal when my pennies were declining. Today he insisted on providing an extra special lunch for you."

"That's why the portions are so great and the price so reasonable?"

"Yes, Martha."

"We should thank him," Mrs. Freeman said.

"No, just tell him how much you enjoyed the food. Trust me, that will be thanks enough."

After lunch Mrs. Freeman voiced the topic that was on her mind. She did so, of course, on behalf of her daughters too.

"Augusta, we read the official *Fair Book*. Beyond your name and a few words about your work there's nothing about your background."

"And you would like to know more?"

"Yes."

"What would you to know?"

"Start with your childhood," Rachel said with emphasis.

"My childhood…I was born in Green Cover Springs in 1882. That's in Florida near Jacksonville. My full name was Augusta Christine Fells. I was the 7th of 14 children. My father was Edward Fells, a Methodist Minister. My mother was Cornelia Murphy."

"Such a large family."

"Too much for any mother, I'm afraid, Martha."

"How did you get involved with sculpting?"

"It began when I was a child. We lived a little out of town. Our home was built on lovely red clay. As a child I would grab a fistful of the stuff and make small animals out of the clay. It came so naturally to me, or should I say to my hands. I really couldn't help myself. I molded images and told myself stories about them. They kind of took on a life of their own."

"Like playing with dolls?"

"All my life, I think."

BUSY HANDS

"Something like that, Rachel. But, of course, it did get me into trouble."

"How was that possible?"

"Martha, my father was very strict. The *Bible* was the foundation of his life. He considered my toy clay animals 'graven images' and sinful. On more than one occasion he tried to whip the art out of me. Usually four or five times a week…"

"How awful."

"Nevertheless, Mrs. Freeman, I persevered. I was headstrong. After awhile he sort of gave up. In high school the principal took a liking to me. He was attracted to my youthful efforts to mold clay into something of beauty. He encouraged me to teach a modeling class. That was in West Palm Beach. Can you beat that, a high school girl teaching a class?"

"Sounds like your principal recognized your youthful talent. Things were looking up for you, it seems."

"Rachel, I thought so but then things got complicated. I met John T. Moore in 1907. We married and soon after my daughter Irene Connie Moore was born in 1906. I was about 16 at the time."

"Young and with a family."

"Yes, Mrs. Freeman, at least for a short time. My husband died soon after Irene was born. A few years later I married James Savage. The marriage didn't work out and we divorced in the 1920's. I did, however, keep his name. In 1923, I married Robert Lincoln Poston. He was a protégé of Marcus Garvey."

"The Marcus Garvey who strutted around in an embellished uniform and wanted Blacks to return to Africa?"

MARCUS GARVEY

"That's right. On behalf of Garvey my husband traveled to Liberia. He died of pneumonia aboard a ship while returning home. I haven't married since."

"Your formal training...When did that begin?"

"I guess in 1919. I was granted a booth at the Palm Beach Country Fair. I was awarded a $25 prize and a beautiful blue ribbon for the most original exhibit. The judging officials also gave me a letter of recommendation for an artist in New York City. His name was Solon Borglum."

FAIR FACTS

Solon Borglum was an American sculptor who was noted for his depiction of frontier life, including cowboys and Native Americans. He was the younger brother of Gutzon Borglum and uncle of Lincoln Borglum. These two men were responsible for the creation of the carvings at Mount Rushmore.

SOLON BORGLUM

————————

"I wanted to go to the American School of Sculpture. However, I couldn't afford the tuition. Borglum encouraged me to apply to the Cooper Union. This was a scholarship-based school in New York. I was admitted in 1921. I'm happy to say that I was selected before 142 men, who were on the waiting list. Fortunately, my work impressed the Cooper Union Advisory Council and I was given funds for my room and board. I completed the four-year degree program in three years. After graduation I headed to Harlem and became part of what was later called the Harlem Renaissance. At the time I worked in a Manhattan steam laundry to support myself and Irene."

"But you were on your way?"

"Yes, but not without more complications. My father's home was destroyed by a hurricane. He had a stroke. My folks moved in with me in my small West 135th apartment. So there I was… 29 years old… Thrice married … Widowed and divorced… And now caring for my parents… It was almost too much."

"You're a survivor, Augusta."

"Yes, I think I am, Rachel. Black women must be survivors, don't you think?"

The question resonated with the women. Its implications were all too evident. Black women brought to the table the glue that maintained Black family life and traditions. They had to be strong and resilient.

"Things did improve. I received commissions to do a bust of W.E.B. DuBois. This work led to more commissions, including a bust of Marcus Garvey and one of William Pickens, Sr. who was important in the NAACP. The critics said, "I depicted Negroes in a more humane, neutral way, as opposed to stereotypes of the time."

BREAKING FROM STEREOTYPES

"Do you have a favorite work?"

Augusta paused, considered the question and then reached into her purse. She took out a small Kodak snapshot. She explained, "This is one closest to my heart." She handed the photo to Mrs. Freeman who shared it with her daughters.

"I called it Gamin. My nephew sat for me. Along with the rest of the family he had come to New York to be with me after the hurricane. His name was Ellis. It took me over 48-hours to complete this project."

"Ellis looks like the kid, any kid in the neighborhood, just a nice looking boy," Ms. Freeman remarked.

"Why do you call this work Gamin?" Rachel asked. "It's a new word for me."

"I spent some time in France where I picked up some of the language. In French gamin means street urchin or an imp, an innocent character given to pranks and a bit of mischievousness with a degree of street smartness."

"Sounds like our brother," Martha said. "He's given to silly pranks and a bit of foolishness."

"Perhaps it's a stage the boys have to go through."

"You may be right, dear daughter."

"Augusta, you mentioned living in France. What was that all about?"

"Rachel, it's not a happy story."

————————

FAIR FACTS

In 1923, Augusta Savage was accepted to a summer program at the Fontainebleau Fine Arts School in France. After her application was accepted the American selection committee discovered she was Black. Her acceptance was revoked. She was deeply hurt by this but refused to take this decision without a fight. She challenged the committee openly and mainly through the *New York World,* a Black newspaper, and even papers in Paris. One of the people who took up her cause was W.E.B. DuBois, the Black scholar who was founder and editor of the NAACP's *Crisis* magazine. Direct appeals were made to the French government but to no avail. She never got the appointment.

————————

"I came home from France deeply disappointed and quite depressed. The thought that my race would keep me from improving my skills was quite painful."

"That certainly wasn't fair, Augusta."

"Fairness can be an elusive commodity, Rachel."

"What did you do?"

"Martha, I had to stop feeling sorry for myself. I got on with my work and then the Great Depression hit. Art sales were difficult. Commissions were hard to come by. However, in 1934, I became the first Black artist elected to the National Association of Women Painters and Sculptors. A little later I launched a project deep to my heart, the Augusta Savage Studio of Arts and Crafts. I found a location in Harlem that I could afford --- West 143rd Street. I was most fortunate with the funding. The Carnegie Foundation provided me with a grant."

"You were now a teacher."

"Right, Martha. The Studio was open to anyone who wanted to paint, draw, or sculpt. Modestly my studio prospered. In 1937, I became the director of the Harlem Community Art Center. I received some assistance from the New Deal's Works Progress Administration program to help artists. Over 1,500 people participated in the workshops."

"You really reached a lot of people."

"I did, Mrs. Freeman, and then one day some special people reached out to me."

"You're going to tell us who, aren't you?"

"After a lingering sip of lemonade, yes."

FAIR FACTS

In 1935 Eleanor Roosevelt visited the Harlem Community Art Center. As the eyes and ears of the president she was checking out a New Deal program to assist artists. This was the Federal Arts Project. Mrs. Roosevelt attended the inauguration of the Center. In the photograph shown below she is with four female Black artists. Standing left to right, Louise Jefferson, Sara West, Gwendolyn Bennett, Augusta Savage, and Mrs. Roosevelt.

The first lady found the Center well run and applauded Augusta for her work. Moreover, she used the Center as a model for other art programs across the country. Augusta Savage had provided a pathway for Black artists. She taught them. She gave them the tools to find work. She was a mentor to many, including Gwendolyn Knight and Norman Lewis.

GWENDOLYN KNIGHT AND HER WORK

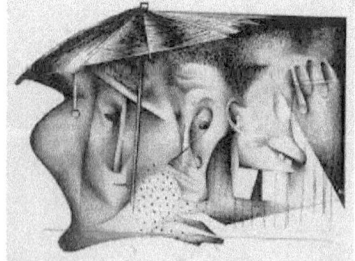

NORMAN LEWIS AND HIS WORK

"What a thrill to meet Mrs. Roosevelt."

"One of the highlights of my life, Rachel. She took a real interest in what we were doing, always asking what the government could do to provide increased assistance. To her credit she had a keen eye for artistic expression in its varied forms. She enjoyed chitchatting with the art students. She seemed right at home in Harlem."

"I would have loved to meet her, Augusta."

"Perhaps someday you will, Martha, especially if you get involved in politics. The next presidential election looms in November. The Republicans will challenge the New Deal programs in 1940."

As the fates would have it the proprietor appeared at their table. Always amiable and adorned with a beguiling smile Ralph was carrying a large tray holding, as it turned out, four plates, each covered with a sparkling white napkin.

"Ladies, something special, hot apple pie right out of the oven. Compliments of my wife…" That said, he removed the napkins, saying, "A scoop of vanilla ice cream is available if you're interested."

"Ralph, you must thank your wife."

"It was her pleasure, Augusta. As to the ice cream?"

The women considered the offer but declined the overture. The large slices of pie seemed sufficient, though the temptation was difficult to deny. At that point, Ralph left, tray in hand, saying, "Enjoy." This they did, even as their conversation continued.

"Augusta, how did you end up in the Fair?"

"Martha, I applied for a commission from the Board of Design to be included in the New York World's Fair. It was as simple as that. Fortunately, four women were accepted. I was one of them. I was commissioned to create a sculpture showcasing the impact that Blacks have had on music. This led to my effort --- *Life Every Voice and Sing.* That effort soon came to be known as *The Harp.* I had hoped it would communicate my desire to promote Black arts and the Black Community. In that sense the work was an activist sculpture."

"We certainly think you succeeded, Augusta."

"You're most kind, Mrs. Freeman."

Suddenly Rachel started laughing, catching everyone with a 'Why are you laughing' look.

"I was just wondering how Dad and James are getting along with the man of steel!"

"Dad, look at the size of the crowd."

"Lots of people want to see Superman, James."

"There must be 3,000 people here."

"Well, Macy's Toyland and Superman, Incorporated have been pushing this day. You know, come and see Superman in the flesh."

"And not just him, Dad. Batman and Robin too."

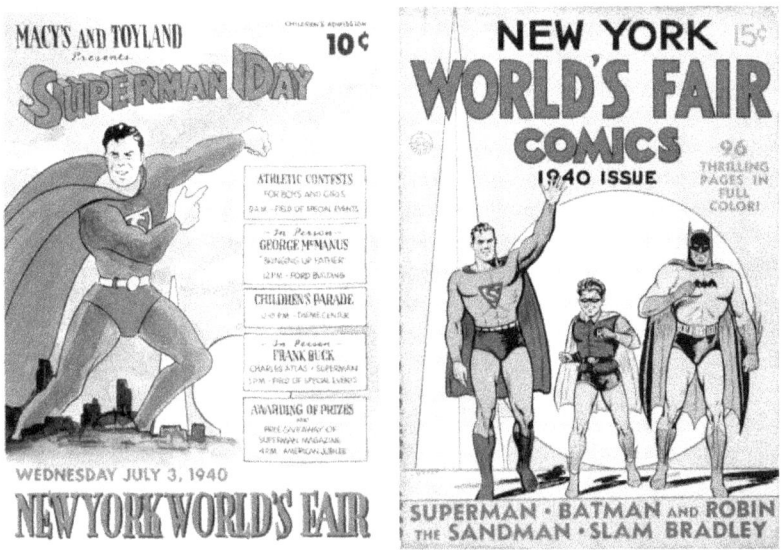

PROMOTING SUPERMAN DAY

"There's going to be competitions for the kids --- races, rope-skipping contests to determine a Super-Boy and a Super-Girl."

"Want to compete, James?"

"No way. That's for little kids."

"I hear the judges will include Charles Atlas, the body builder, and Ray Middleton, the Broadway performer who dresses up in a Superman outfit."

"That's the guy I want to see."

"Well then, James, look over there."

RAY MIDDLETON AS SUPERMAN

Standing on a pedestal high over the crowd was Superman. From his stance and swagger it was obvious that Superman had muscles and toughness, just the person to protect the Fair guests from any bad guys. The comics proved that point.

SUPERMAN SAVES THE NEW YORK WORLD'S FAIR

"James, look over there, over to your left. Isn't that Joe Shuster? Isn't that the guy who draws the cartoons?"

"And check who is next to him, Dad. That's Jerry Siegel. He does all the writing. Wouldn't it be great if we could get an autograph?"

JERRY SIEGEL STANDING, JOE SHUSTER SITTING

With the help of his father nicely elbowing their way through the crowd they reached Siegel and Shuster. Before they could get autographs another man approached them. This turned out to be Jack Liebowitz, the founder of D.C. Comics.

"You guys came out for Superman Day?"

"My kid loves your comic books."

"Well, how about some free copies, and with a little help from me, perhaps an autograph or two. What'd you think?"

"That would be great."

"Here take these. I need you to keep up on Lois Lane, Perry White, and Jimmy Olson. They're always getting into trouble. They make the guy from Krypton work overtime."

"I think I've read every edition, Mr. Liebowitz."

"Keep it up kid. That helps our bottom line. Now let's get those autographs."

A few minutes later James was the happiest kid at the Fair. He was even happier when his father handed him a special D.C. edition --- *New York World's Fair Comics.*

Somewhere in his youthful heart James heard the words that kept young people anticipating the next edition of Superman, or glued to their radio.

Faster than a speeding bullet, more powerful than a locomotive, able to leap tall buildings in a single bound...Look! Up in the sky! It's a bird. It's a plane. It's Superman!

"Dad, I wonder how they ever came up with Superman?"

"I guess it started with the Greeks and their mythological gods. We'll need to ask your mom about that."

"Dad, something has been puzzling me."

"And that is?"

"None of the superheroes are Black. Why is that?"

––––––––––––

FAIR FACTS

Superman is the archetype of the superhero as understood and reflected in a white culture, as it was in the 1930's and 1940's. The "man of steel" represented a white world and its values. Racial stereotyping founds its way into the comics. That was the case. White male characters dominated. They were the main characters. Without question, minorities were under represented. This included women.

Where present, people of color were often shown as from the lower socioeconomic strata compared to the main white characters. In short, comics are representative of prevailing white cultural ideas during the Golden Age of Comics. That being said, the superhero always has a mysterious past. Where was he born? Where is his home? How did he get here? He also has unique skills and weaknesses. He is a powerful force. He can, however, be destroyed by a fatal flaw that he has little control over. His powers are given to him or he can be born with them. Always he tries to use his powers for the greater good; that is, to help those in need of his unusual talents. That being the case he must always have a nemesis, a sort of equal and opposite entity that tests the superhero. And one other thing... The superhero usually has some sort of outlandish outfit. That's a prerequisite.

SUPER HEROES

————————

"Dad, everyone in Smallville is white. How can that be? Even with Batman and Robin... I never see a Black face in the comics. I never see myself."

Every father has a moment when no answer will fully suffice. Mr. Freeman knew that as he considered James' question and statement. What could he tell his son? He could not evade his son's inquisitiveness.

He was forced to speak to the realities of life, a Black living within a white culture. He took his son aside. They found a somewhat quiet spot in the food court, and over root beer they talked. That meant the father spoke, the son questioned, and the cycle of Q and A was repeated again and again. In the end Mr. Freeman could only say, "And, James, that's the way it is."

"I don't like it."

"I agree but we must live with some things."

"Can't things change?"

"They can and have, but perhaps a bit slower than we would prefer."

"I need to think about what you said."

"Yes, you should. You're no longer a boy. You must take on the responsibilities of a man to think and consider. Do you understand?"

"Yes."

"Good. Now let's talk about an exception to the rule."

"What?"

"Mandrake the Magician."

FAIR FACTS

Mandrake the Magician was a comic strip that first appeared in 1934. It was created by Lee Falk and was syndicated by King Features. Comic strip historians consider Mandrake the Magician the first superhero. Mandrake is a magician whose power comes from his ability to use "unusually fast hypnotic techniques" to stymie gangsters, mad scientists, and extraterrestrials. Mandrake also has other powers, including the ability to become invisible, or to levitate. Even his clothes have magical powers --- his hat, cloak, and wand. Mandrake lives in Xanadu, a mansion atop a mountain in New York State. His home has high-tech equipment that includes a closed circuit television.

What makes the comic strip unusual is that Mandrake has a Black assistant, who is his best friend, crime fighting companion, and in many ways his equal. His name is Lothar and he's not just a guy off the streets. Mandrake met him in Africa where he was the Prince of the Seen Nations, a "mighty federation of jungle tribes." Rather than becoming the King he follows Mandrake on his adventures around the world. Lothar is no ordinary being. He also has magical powers. He is "impervious to heat and cold." He possesses the stamina of a thousand men. He is capable of lifting an elephant by one hand. More than an assistant he is a key element in Mandrake's success. He is a partner, not a subservient. Though Mandrake wears formal attire, a very civilized tuxedo and Lothar dresses in a native leopard garb befitting royalty, their fashions do not suggest a sense of inequality.

Lothar was the first serious Black comic book character. He was not present for mere comic relief. His relationship with Mandrake pushed against the usual stereotyping where a white character always leading a Black character out of danger. That business was a metaphor accepted by most whites that Black people needed the help of whites to advance themselves. On many occasions it is Mandrake who must be saved by Lothar as shown on a comic book cover.

––––––––––

"Dad, I need to read *Mandrake the Magician*."
"Yes, you do."

"I wonder if there will ever be a Black superhero standing alone in a comic book."

"If the followers of Lothar have their way, yes."

"Where to now, Dad?"

"*Jungleland*, but first a surprise."

Mr. Freeman handed his son a large brown envelope, saying only, "For a special son."

James quickly opened the envelope and then hugged his father, saying to him, "I always wanted this."

THE FIRST EDITION OF SUPERMAN – JUNE, 1938

——————————

About 1938, Frank Buck was invited to participate in the 1939 New York World's Fair. The famous American hunter, animal collector, and author agreed to bring his jungle camp to New York. Already famous as the "Bring 'em Back Alive" celebrity, he brought *Jungleland* to the Fair. His exhibit showcased thousands of rare specimens of birds, reptiles, and wild animals, including Jiff, a five-year old trained orangutan. He also brought a trio of performing elephants. One particularly unusual exhibit was an 80-foot "monkey island," where over 600 monkeys delighted visitors with their antics.

FRANK BUCK ON AN ELEPHANT IN JUNGLELAND

Over two millions visitors viewed Frank Buck's *Jungleland* and the thrilling exhibits and rides. Without a doubt it was one of the Fair's greatest attractions.

WRESTLING AN ALLIGATOR   RIDING A CAMEL

Jungleland provided many jobs for Blacks. That was, of course, a good thing. There was, however, criticism of the type of jobs offered to people of color. Almost always they played African natives. That being the case they were dressed in jungle outfits and were portrayed as semi-civilized natives brought to America by Frank Buck. For the critics of the Fair employment policies an element of racism seemed present.

BLACKS ACTING AS NATIVES

"Dad, Frank Buck sure knows how to put on a show."

"Including great rides, James. You looked pretty good on the elephant."

"For a moment I thought I was in Africa."

"Not Harlem?"

"Africa."

FAIR VISITORS ON AN ELEPHANT RIDE

"Where to now, Dad."

"Let's catch up with the family and head home."

"Tomorrow?"

"A surprise."

"Okay, I think we're about ready to start."

"Mom, did you pack the extra sandwiches, our emergency stash if we run out of greenbacks?"

"You won't go hungry, James."

"The weather looks good according to the paper. It will be humid. No need for our umbrella and heavier jackets."

"A light jacket might to best, Rachel."

"And good walking shoes. We're going to see a lot of things today."

"Martha, very prudent. No sandals, especially those open toed ones."

"Dad, you have our itinerary?"

That question need not be asked. Mr. Freeman always planned each day at the Fair. It wasn't that he was a control-type person, though he wasn't against being in charge. Planning for him was important for three reasons: First, transportation to the Fair had to be accounted for, timing and costs. Second, food at the Fair ranged from modest to expensive, and with a family of five eating costs added up quickly. Third, some money had to be set aside for souvenirs and park rides. That being the case the day's itinerary was important.

"Yes, I have it. Today we're going to the Transportation Zone to learn about the newest technologies and the joy of trains. All aboard."

"Do we see Augusta today?"

"Hopefully after we see the Futurama Exhibit in the GM Pavilion."

"Well, let's get going, Dad. We don't want to almost miss the IND again."

"James, you are the impatient one."

———————————

FAIR FACTS

The New York World's Fair catered to millions of visitors. This led to two problems. First, once in the Fair how do you transport them around the vast acreage? Second, how do you get millions to the Fair in the first place? Parking at the Fair was limited to 35,000 cars and 575 buses. If you didn't drive or hitch a Greyhound ride how did you get to the Fair? The answer cost $1.7 million dollars. A special World's Fair railroad had to be built. It was called the World's Fair Line. It was a temporary branch of the Independent Subway System (IND). A new train station was built in New York City. Along with two other companies, the Inter-Borough Rapid Transit and the Brooklyn Manhattan Transit, passengers were whisked from the City to the Fair. This was a major project. Marshy swampland in the line's right-of-way had to be filled in and a large trestle bridge was needed over a landfill. At the northern terminus a large train station was built with 18 turnstiles to accommodate traffic in both directions. Over 7,000,000 customers used the system in 1939. The cost was 10-cents to use the line. The first run occurred on April 30, 1939 and the last train departed the Fair on October 28, 1940.

There were ten entrances to the Fair. On site there were 100 Greyhound buses to ferry people at 10-cents per person. There were also tractor trains at 35-cents per adult and 15-cents were child. For those who walked the Fair built 50,000 benches to rest tired feet.

FOR TIRED FEET

111

After entering the Fair the Freeman family gathered themselves, which really meant checking out their go-to map. In this case it meant checking out the Communication Zone.

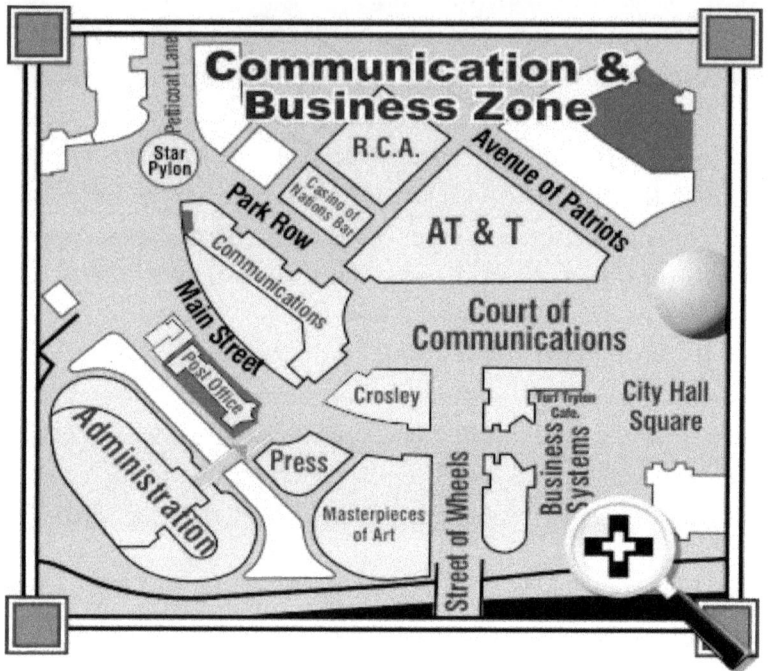

"Let's head for the AT&T Pavilion."

"Dad, I hear the Bell System provides free long distance calls."

"That's what I've heard too, Rachel."

"Maybe we can make a call."

"Martha, who should we call?"

"Her boyfriend in Brooklyn," James added with a flourish.

"No way. The calls aren't private. You're connected to a special headset and anyone can listen in on this amazing technology."

"So Martha, don't say anything too personal."

Martha made her phone call. The family pretended not to listen. Other visitors paid no attention at all.

"Well, did you speak to Mr. Perfect, Martha?"

"James, he wasn't home. I spoke to his mother."

"Imagine talking over such long distances."

"Unbelievable, Martha."

"What did you think, dear?"

"I thought those great doors to the AT&T exhibit were out of this world. Think of it… Doors that were fifty feet tall, colored in warm Deco colors."

THE GREAT DOORS

"And the two figures were something, Mom. Each one was 20-feet tall. The one on the left door depicted a telephone lineman. The one on the right showed a telephone operator. No phone call without those indispensible people."

"Yes, they were something, Rachel."

"Lots of jobs binding the nation with telephone lines. Some for the guys, some for the ladies."

"A division of labor or so it seems, Dad."

It was James who brought up the subject again.

"All the pictures in the exhibit only showed white people doing those things. Why are we always left out?"

James' query was left unanswered.

————————————

The next stop for the Freeman family was the RCA Pavilion. There they saw a new form of radio transmitting. It was called FM (frequency modulation) and was being made public for the first time. In addition, the exhibit was lit with fluorescent lighting. All were amazed by it compared to a light bulb. And then they saw another new invention that really took them by surprise. It was a kind of magic. It was called a facsimile or FAX machine. It could transmit an 8-inch by 12-inch newspaper at a rate of one page per eighteen minutes from one location to another. Their common response was, "How do they do that?

"With that machine I could write a letter to grandma Lucy without using a postage stamp. That's something."
"Yes, dear, but two machines would be necessary. Don't forget that. One to send and one to receive."

————————————

The family then moved on to the National Cash Register (NCR) exhibit. They were pushed along by James, who said, "I want to see the world's largest cash register."

And they did… The register had 2½ foot numbers. The exhibit included a display of all 7,857 parts of a modern cash register.

"Dad, I wonder how big a dime must be for that thing?"

"Good question, Rachel. Paper currency would be like a small blanket."

"That's sounds okay. You know, going to sleep covered with a dollar bill. Very comforting considering our budget."

"Dear wife, you'd probably pull most of George Washington to your side of the bed."

"I still like the old fashioned cash register. It's like a fine piece of jewelry."

"No question about that, Martha."

THE OLD AND THE NEW

"James, doesn't the exhibit remind you of that giant typewriter we saw yesterday?" Rachel asked.

"You bet."

THE GIANT UNDERWOOD TYPEWRITER

The Freeman family moved on to the Kodak Pavilion where they were introduced to Kodachrome, a color film available in two types: regular for day use and Type A for dim or artificial light. The company claimed that the dyes in the new film did not fade over time unlike their competitors. The Kodak mantra was: "You and your camera are cordially invited to the New York World's Fair." Of course, in 1939 movie cameras were still expensive, especially when it came to making a movie or having your own dark room. Only the really affluent could afford to do that. As a point of fact a 16mm Kodak camera cost about $1800 in today's dollars. However, there was another less expensive option. The Kodak Company came out with a special edition. It was called the "Bullet" camera and it sold for $2.25. Still photos only… If you wanted a better camera the "Brownie" camera sold for $2.75. Once you purchased a camera, visitors could go into the Kodak-Photo Garden. It featured a number of snapshot ready tableaux.

THE PEOPLE'S CAMERA

"Dad, how about it? Let's buy a Brownie."
"James, that's a big piece of change."
"But we could use it at the Fair and at home."
"I don't know, Martha."
"It's a one time purchase. Come on, Dad."
"I…"
"Mom, speak to him," Rachel said in a determined voice.
"Dear. Let's splurge, just this one time."

And that's how the Freeman family got a Brownie camera. It came in handy at their next stop.

———————————————

"Wow, look at that thing. Get the camera ready, Dad. We'll stand in front of it."

The Freeman family congregated, and with the help of a friendly Fair visitor, had their picture taken in front of the Carrier Cone. At a cost of $200,000 the five-story building was devoted exclusively to the virtues of air-conditioning. The building was dubbed the "Igloo of Tomorrow." Both the inside and outside of the building were coated with a sparkling white stucco to imitate snow. On the inside walls the Northern Lights were projected in a central exhibition space. In addition, there were displays of air-conditioning equipment and a tribute to Willis Carrier, the founder of the company. At the entrance to the building there were two 48-foot thermometers. One showed Nature's temperature outside the Carrier Cone, the other indicated the temperature inside --- 90 degrees outside, 70 degrees inside. Those numbers got people's attention.

THE CARRIER CONE

FAIR FACTS

Before air-conditioning it could be difficult to work or sleep when the temperature ranged high and moisture was in the air, creating humid conditions. As the story goes Willis Carrier was standing on a Pittsburgh train platform in 1902. Due to the foggy day there was a great deal of mist. Carrier realized that if he could take dry air and pass it through water to create fog, this would make it possible to manufacture air with specific amounts of moisture in it. It took him almost a year to complete his invention, permitting him to control humidity, which is the key to air-conditioning.

WILLIS CARRIER AND HIS INVENTION

Years later the Carrier Corporation pulled off a stunt on the last day of the 1939 New York World's Fair, October 31st. The company got a full-blooded Eskimo family to ride a dog sled at the Carrier Cone. The family was led by Mayokok and had participated in other events during the summer. The publicity effort was to show the family bedding down for the winter in the igloo. What was not said publically was that the family was part of an Amusement Zone display of "backward" or "exotic people." Critics called it pseudo-anthropological science to illustrate, by contrast, white progress in making the modern world.

In doing so, as the argument went, the contributions of others were muted, if even expressed at the Fair.

———————————

"Where to next?"
"Martha, in a word, Futurama."
"And more photos."

CHAPTER 11 – FUTURAMA

Mr. Freeman, as always, checked his Fair map for the Transportation Zone. He was looking for the General Motors Pavilion and an exhibit called Futurama. He found it sandwiched between the Goodrich and Firestone tire companies, and adjacent to the Ford complex.

"Follow me."

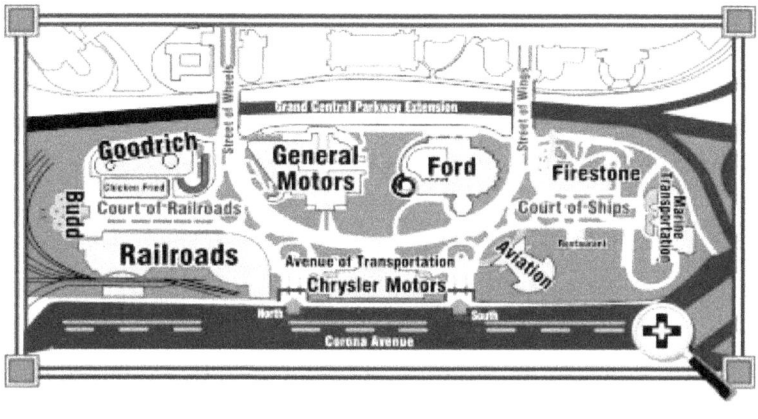

FAIR FACTS

General Motors sponsored Futurama, one of the most well attended venues in the 1939 New York World's Fair. It was both an exhibit and a ride. It presented a view of a possible world some 20 years into the future --- that is, to the 1960's. The exhibit was designed by Norman Bel Geddes based on his 1937 Shell Oil *City of Tomorrow*, a model city. That proved to be the prototype for a far larger rendering of a futuristic city for the 1939 Fair. Geddes described his work as such:

Futurama is a large-scale model representing almost every type of terrain in America and illustrating how a motorway system may be laid down over the entire country --- across mountains, over rivers and lakes, through cities and past towns --- never deviating from a direct course and always adhering to our basic principles of highway design: safety, comfort, speed, and economy.

What Geddes did was to introduce his concept of what might be called an interstate highway system.

GEDDES PLANNING THE FUTURE

The large-scale model was indeed that. One acre was needed for the display. The model included 500,000 individually designed buildings, a million trees representing 13 different species. About 50,000 model cars were part of the project; 10,000 of them traveled along a 14-lane multi-speed highway system.

1937   1939

BUILDING THE MODEL FUTURE

———————————

"Hang on, everyone."

"For dear life," Rachel responded to her brother.

The Freeman family, along with over 500 other visitors, was seated and prepared for an 18-minute ride on a conveyor system that would transport them along a ½-mile winding path through the model. As they traveled along there were light shows, sounds, and color effects to enhance the experience. The ride moved at glacial speed, 120-feet per minute or 1.36 mph. This allowed the riders to look down through a continuous curved pane of glass towards the model. The virtue of this elevated position permitted spectators to see multiple aspects of the model. They could view city blocks in proportion to a highway system. Over 400 topographical sections could be viewed based on photographs of different regions of the country. The Fairchild Aircraft Company provided the photographs.

Business Week described the popularity of the venue this way:

More than 30,000 persons daily, the show's capacity, inched along the sizzling pavement in long queues until they reached the chairs, which transported them to a tourist's paradise. It unfolded a prophecy of cities, towns, and rural areas served by a comprehensive road system.

"What a ride!" James said as the family exited the Futurama exhibit. "That people moving conveyor was really something."

"Providing each of us with sound was nice. Even Dad didn't have to ask, 'What did he say?'"

"Martha, what about the souvenir booklet each of us received?" Rachel added. "All Dad had to do was read a written version of the narration as we traveled along."

"I admit the booklet really helped. Futurama's imaginary landscape of what things would look like in the 1960's was most helpful. It gave all of us a glimpse of the future."

"I hope the future includes us?"

"What are you getting at, James?"

"Just this."

James held up a brochure put out by the Westinghouse Company.

"Where did you get that?" Mrs. Freeman asked.
"Some guy was passing them out."
"So what did you mean by your question?"
"Mom, look at the picture. All the people are white. The guy didn't have any brochures with a Black family. That's what he told me."

James was on to something. The brochure showed the cheery Middleton family. There was Babs and Brad, each overflowing with the exuberance of 18 and 19 year olds "romping through wonderland like two kittens across a rug," or so explained the Westinghouse advertisement. There was "Father Tom" and "Mother Jane" calmly enjoying the Fair. Grandma was also seen as she remembered other Fairs and an earlier time. Westinghouse claimed that the Middleton family represented the typical American family from "Everywhere USA." This wholesome family was fun-loving, a "family of folks you know, friends who live just around the cover from everyone."

"James, this is just an ideal family, a sort of glorified image of what families should be. They're fictitious."
"Martha, I get that, but why is the ideal family always white. Why not an idealized Black family? Why can't our family live in Futurama's suburbs like the white families?"

James' question hung in the air unanswered. Any answer would prove unsatisfactory and possibly dampen their day at the Fair. Mr. Freeman attempted to find a middle ground. "James, we must hope, as we have in the past, that the future will improve for our family. Leave things at that for the moment."
"But..."
"No more. Let's head for the Casino of Nations Restaurant to meet Augusta and have lunch."

CHAPTER 12 – RAILROADS ON PARADE

"Do you believe this menu?" Rachel said a bit apprehensively. "Roast Spring Lamb, $1.25."

"And Fried Filet," Martha quickly injected, "$1.20. That's a lot for Dad's budget."

"A Hot Turkey Sandwich with mashed potatoes costs $1.00," James pointed out. "Same for a Hot Roast Beef Sandwich."

The Freeman Family was dining at the Casino of Nations Restaurant, a nice place to eat or rest, or some combination of the two. The restaurant was huge. The seating capacity was more than 1,500. An additional 250 seats were outside and on shaded grounds and this was where the family caught up with Augusta Savage. To his credit Mr. Freeman listened to his children discuss the pricy menu without a hint of his feelings. Of course, Mrs. Freeman knew what was going through his mind. "Maybe we'll just have a ham sandwich at $.50 or some Chicken salad at $.60. Throw in coffee or tea at $.15 or a bottle of Grade A milk at $.20 and we might survive this place." The musings of the parents came to an end when Augusta spoke.

"Did I mention the restaurant owners love *The Harp*. In fact, I made a miniature replica for them as a keepsake once the Fair ends. In their appreciation I always get a meal at half-price, as do my friends this particular day."

No nicer words could have been spoken. Mr. Freeman breathed a sigh of relief, and everyone plucked a menu item that they most wanted. For the parents that meant Broiled Fresh Spring Chicken... As for Augusta she laid claim to Broiled Salisbury Steak with mushroom sauce.

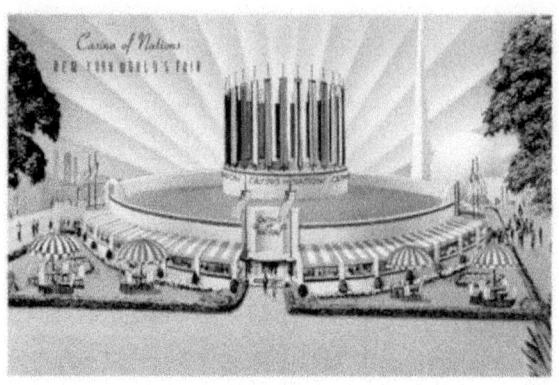

CASINO OF NATIONS RESTAURANT

"Augusta, how can we thank you?"

"No need, Mrs. Freeman. We're family, are we not?"

"We are."

"You'll stay with us when you're in Harlem."

"Rachel, I will take you up on that. Now let me tell you what you're going to see. First, we'll go to the Railroad Building. It's quite a structure. It looks like a gigantic railroad roundhouse where locomotives are stored and serviced, along with passenger cars. The latest streamlined trains of America and Europe will be on display. There will also be some famous locomotives in our history including, I might add, a dramatization of the building of the transcontinental rail road."

"I can't wait."

"Finish your meal first, James."

"Mom…"

"And all your vegetables before devouring your dessert. That's an order."

At that everyone laughed, even James, if not a bit shyly.

Augusta then added, "Remember all of this is part of what the Fair officials call *Railroads on Parade*. It's in the Railway Building."

Railroad Building

New York World's Fair 1939

THE RAILROAD BUILDING

FAIR FACTS

The *Railroads on Parade* venue was viewed in a 3,000-seat theater with a cast of 250 employees within the Railroad Building. A diorama greeted visitors. It was huge, 160 feet wide and 40 feet deep. The building also contained miniature railroads with more than 500 pieces of rolling stock. These small trains traveled through cities, towns, and villages, across bridges and through tunnels. They passed farms and factories. To do all this, some 3,388 feet of "O" gauge track was used. Added to all of this was 1,000 miniature buildings, 6,000 tiny trees, 7,000 gallons of water, and 300,000 feet of wire for the control systems.

The parade reenacted the progress of rail transportation from the 1820's through 1939. The goal of the show was to briefly tell the story of railroads through a series of staged presentations with narration and appropriate music. An official program contained the following introductory paragraph:

Into every corner of our social and economic existence, the railroad is tightly interwoven. It is the backbone of the country; no, even more, it is its veritable lifeblood. In its 250,000 miles of steel veins, it flows to every far corner of far-flung land, it binds in its living, throbbing embrace city and town and village, the open country, the forest, the mine, the forge, the factory, and the sea. It is indeed the nation's lifeblood, the great arm not only of its industry, but of its military defense. If it were to die, then the nation would die.

––––––––––––––

A thin as a rail gentlemen appeared before the visitors. As one might have expected he wore an engineer's hat and overalls with suspenders that covered his blacker than night cotton shirt. Holding a microphone in one hand and flourishing a small breaking flag in the other he got down to business.

"It's May 10, 1869. The place is Promontory Point, Utah. Two railroads, having crossed the nation finally meet. The Union Pacific's long trek across the 'fruited plains' of the West from Omaha, Nebraska was over, as was the Central Pacific's difficult climb over the Sierra Nevada Mountains after leaving Sacramento, California. Taking front stage, Leland Stanford of California hammered in a 17.6-karat "golden spike" to nail down the last rail to symbolize the uniting of the country by steel rails."

UNITING THE COUNTRY BY RAILS, 1869   REENACTING THE MOMENT

The family next moved on to the locomotive exhibit. That meant looking at the PRR S-1.

PRR S-1

The PRR S-1 was a steam engine display that actually stayed in place while running continuously at 6-mph on a dynamometer that measured mechanical force or the driving torque of a rotating machine. Sleek and powerful in appearance the PRR S-1 suggested contained energy, which, if released would pull a hundred railroad cars.

The Freemans next moved over to the *Coronation Scot*. It was built in 1937 for the coronation of King George VI and Queen Elizabeth. At the time it was one of the most powerful steam engines in the world, achieving speeds up to 114 mph. It lived up to its reputation as an express passenger train of the London, Midland and Scottish Railway.

THE CORONATION SCOT

Almost immediately the family came across an EMU. James was overjoyed to see one. His sisters didn't grasp at first why he was so interested. Their parents stepped aside and let the siblings work things out. As for Augusta, she simply chuckled.

"Okay, James, what's the big deal? What's an EMU?"
"Martha, the letters stand for 'electric multiple unit.'"
"Meaning?"
"Meaning it doesn't have a locomotive. It uses electricity as the motive power. Electric traction motors are incorporated into one or more of the passenger cars."

"No coal?"

"No coal."

"No crude oil?"

"No crude oil."

"That's different. How fast can it go?"

"Susan, as fast as traditional locomotive powered trains according to the Italians who have the most EMU's."

AN EMU IN ITALY

The locomotive display didn't elicit the interest of James' sisters. They were looking at a replica of Peter Coopers' locomotive called the Tom Thumb. It was the first American-built steam locomotive to operate in the US. That was back in 1829. Cooper constructed it to convince the owners of the newly formed Baltimore and Ohio Railroad (B&O) to use steam engines. Cooper designed a four-wheel locomotive with a vertical boiler and vertically mounted cylinders that drove the wheel on one of the axles. The engine was powered by anthracite coal. Rudimentary as it was the Tom Thumb marked the beginning of America's love of the rails.

THE TOM THUMB STEAM LOCOMOTIVE

As the Freeman family moved into the great hall of the Railroad Building, Augusta surprised everyone, saying, "Let's meet over in that corner, over by the window where that gentleman is seated."

In a moment they converged as directed where Augusta said, "I asked Professor Silas Jones to join us for reasons that will soon be apparent."

Introductions were made and then Augusta continued. Professor Silas is a good friend and fine academic. Currently he is at Morehouse College in the history department. Now, as to why I invited him to join our little group…I've listened carefully to James' questions in particular concerning the Fair and his questions concerning race. This is an area of Professor Jones' expertise, most specifically as it relates to the nation's railroad history. Professor Jones…"

CHAPTER 13 – THE UNKNOWN HISTORY

Professor Silas Jones was of minimum height and weight with a perpetual stern look to his demeanor and certainly with his words. He quickly provided a personal synopsis.

"I've been at Morehouse for over a decade. It's true I'm in the history department and that I have a penchant for railroad history. Indeed, most of my research has been to uncover and disclose the unknown history of Black contributions to the nation's railroads. More than that I am most interested in the on-going issue of civil rights and trade unionism. And that's why I'm here today. It appears you have a questioning youth at this table, am I not right, James?"

"I…"

"James, what's bothering you about this Fair?"

"I…"

"You what?"

"All the displays…All the exhibits…"

"Yes, what about them?"

"I can't find myself in them."

"Explain yourself, young man."

"I'm not present."

"Spit it out, James. What's bothering you?"

"I'm invisible."

"I can see you."

"That's not what I mean, Professor Jones."

"Well, what do you mean?"

"Blacks don't seem to be at this Fair. Everything seems to be about what white people did, or are doing. I never see a Black face except for someone pushing a broom or sweating over an oven."

"Why is that a problem for you?"

"Because my parents work hard and my sisters are in college…"

"So what?"

"We can do things. We deserve something better at this Fair than just menial work."

"How old are you, James?"

"Sixteen. Well, closer to seventeen."

"And asking good questions. I like that."

The inquisition was over. Professor Silas Jones finally showed a hint of a smile. He turned to the family, saying, "You have a budding civil rights lawyer on your hands. Your good, James, I'm told, on the football field. You ask good questions. There's passion in you. Join your sisters in college. Check out law school. We need Black attorneys fighting for equal rights under the Constitution. You can help make that happen in the courtroom."

Those at the table were quiet. Professor Jones' words had caught them off-guard. Truth be told, the siblings and their parents were delighted to hear the comforting, if not challenging words about James. As for the youngster he was at a loss for words. That wouldn't last long.

Augusta said, "Professor Jones is going to tell you about his invisibility theory and a lot more."

"Blacks are not invisible. That's a myth. We exist. That's a reality. However, all too often our contributions are not recognized, or, if they are, they receive muted coverage. Certainly, racial attitudes and erroneous stereotyping influence what people think of us. Jim Crow is a constant companion. Often our history must be uncovered through hard and persistent research. That being the case I'm like an anthropologist. I must dig to find out what really happened. And that's what we're going to do now. When we're done you'll know we're not invisible. Let's start with George Pullman and his problem."

The Problem

"In 1859 George Pullman was trying to convince the Chicago, Alton, and St. Louis Railroad to permit an experiment. He wanted to convert three old passenger cars into something he called a sleeper car. Though reluctant the company agreed to let Pullman redesign three battered old rail cars. In time Pullman renovated the cars to produce three prototypes: a sleeping car, a parlor car, and a dining car. The new railroad cars were a hit, especially with the affluent who enjoyed the amenities they were accustomed to at home. The good life was now on the rails. However, Pullman had a problem. Can you guess what it was?"

GEORGE PULLMAN

PULLMAN'S SLEEPING CAR

"He needed investment funds?" Rachel asked.

"Yes, but that's not the answer."

"He needed to train people to build and maintain the new cars?" Martha said.

"True, but again I'm looking for another answer."

"He needed railroad companies to buy his new cars?" Mrs. Freeman suggested.

"Of course. Let me provide a hint. The affluent passengers expected special services such as someone to shine their shoes, clean their clothes, take care of the sleeping berths, and serve food in the dining car. These passengers also needed their luggage stowed. Any guesses now?"

"He needed competent workers on the train to provide these services separate from operating the train," Mr. Freeman said in a clear voice. "Perhaps even people who were accustomed to doing such work."

"And who might these workers be, Sir?"

FAIR FACTS

Pullman realized the best possible labor for his new cars would be former slaves, the newly emancipated Blacks. Many were already used to catering to every whim of their former owners. In short, they were already trained to be perfect servants. Pullman made no bones about this. Given the economic conditions of the post-Civil War period, they were willing to work long hours at low wages with little time off. Long hours: up to 400 hours per month. Wages: the worst paid employees of the railroad. Tipping was even built into their wages. This led to the stereotype of the "grinning Uncle Tom," who smiled with sparking white teeth and exaggerated their work in order to garner larger tips. In time, they would be known as porters.

PULLMAN PORTERS

"He was providing low wages for hard work," James declared. "Working 400 hours per month… That was unfair."

"That was the case."

"Focusing on Blacks for this work… Wasn't that racist, Professor?" Martha asked.

"It was. Still there's another side to this business."

"You are justifying it?"

"Heavens no, Rachel. I'm simply explaining something. First, Pullman provided work for those desperately seeking employment. Second, though the work was long and challenging, it was better than the backbreaking work of a field hand tending to crops under the tenant system in the South. Third, though the wages were low, they were still higher than most Blacks were earning in urban areas. Fourth, you were able to travel the country at the company's expense. In time the job of a porter became a coveted position and even generational as father and son worked for Pullman. Working as a porter became a career for some."

"It seems like the porters were trapped," Mr. Freeman said with a harshness to his tone.

"Not completely. Pullman porters became famous for their superior service. In time many fine hotels wanted them, as well as upscale restaurants. A few even found their way into the White House. As an example, J.W. Mays served as President William McKinley's aid in his sleeping car. He went on to serve eight other presidents."

J.W. MAYS

FAIR FACTS

In time the Pullman Palace Car Company only hired Black porters to care for white passengers. Unfortunately, the porters endured constant racism on the job. In many cases they were referred to as "Boy" or "George." The second term was a takeoff on Pullman's first name. To a degree that was the tradeoff: endure racist attitudes for a semi-middle-class life. The relationship was tenuous and couldn't last. In the 1890's something unheard of occurred. A social activist and the publisher of a literary magazine entitled *The Messenger* entered the world of porters. His name was A. Philips Randolph and through his leadership he organized the Brotherhood of Sleeping Car Porters (BSCP).

EMANCIPATING RAILWAY PORTERS

As was the case in the startup of most unions, the Pullman Company resisted unionization of its workers. The fight to organize took over a decade before a collective bargaining contract was signed. Again, this marked the first example of a Black union successfully winning a contract from a major American company. The contract provided for higher wages, more days off, and fewer hours of work.

Over time the new union lent its support to other issues tied to the improvement of Blacks everywhere in the country.

CIVIL RIGHTS MOVEMENT

––––––––––––––

"That's quite a story, Professor Jones."

"James, it's history."

Mr. Freeman gave his wife that special look that sometimes passes between spouses.

"Dear, tell them."

"Tell us what, Mom?" Rachel said in a flurry of words.

"Before he passed away one of our distant relatives was a porter. He worked for the Pullman Company."

"You never told us," Martha said. "Why not?"

"Like much of Black history he simply slipped through the pages of history and maybe my memory."

"We'd like to know more."

"James, after we return home you will."

"Thank you, Professor, for this stimulating information."

"Augusta, I'm not through with young James."

James could only look on wondering what would come next. He didn't have long to wait.

"James, four questions. Number one: where did the phrase, 'I want the real McCoy,' come from? Two: who was the 'Black Edison?' Three: what was the Janney Coupler? Four: what's a water closet?"

James could only stare at the professor with a blank face. As he looked around he noticed his sisters and parents were fixated with the same, 'What are you talking about?' look. Only Augusta seemed undeterred by the questions, almost as if she had insider information.

"At a loss for words, James? No matter. Once more we're going to delve into the notion of 'invisibility.' In this case, however, we will make known what history has brushed aside. And when we do this, I hope you will gain greater insight into our common history."

Question #1: Where did the "Real McCoy" phrase come from? The answer resides in the life of Elijah McCoy. He was another Black who wasn't born in the United States. He was born free on the Ontario shore of Lake Erie in Canada. His parents had fled enslavement in Kentucky and the onerous Fugitive Slave Act. In 1847 he returned to America with his parents and soon became a citizen. Eventually he went to college in Scotland where he earned a certificate as a master mechanical engineer. As the fates would have it, he was unable to practice his trade in Scotland because of racism. He returned to the US and settled in Michigan where he took a position as a fireman and oilman. This was with the Michigan Central Railroad. Being an oilman turned out to be a break for him. Early trains had to stop often so oil could be applied to axles and bearings. This was a dirty and often dangerous job. He reasoned that there could be a better way. What if he could automate the process? This was his goal. In time he invented a lubricating cup that did the job without frequent stops and the personal touch. His invention was an instant hit and soon he had competitors who tried to copy his "cup." Those who worked on trains would have none of it. They always wanted the "real McCoy."

ELIJAH McCOY

———————

Question #2: Who was the "Black Edison?" Granville T. Woods was a prolific inventor. During his lifetime he patented 60 inventions and has been called the "Black Edison." Research indicates that he was the first Black mechanical and electrical engineer after the Civil War. His inventions included an automatic brake for trains, an egg incubator, and a steam boiler furnace. In addition, he developed a device called "telegraphony." It allowed a telegraph station to send voice and telegraph messages through Morse code over a single wire. He also patented the Synchronous Multiplex Railway Telegraph. This allowed communications between train stations from moving trains by creating "a magnetic field around a coiled wire under the trains." This system helped avoid collisions between trains. According to legend Woods always dressed meticulously in black outfits and often referred to himself as an immigrant from Australia, though he was born in Ohio and his mother was Native-American and his father was Black. By telling people he was from Australia he believed he would receive more respect as opposed to being an American Black. The Black newspapers of his day referred to him as the "greatest of Negro inventors." They even referred to him as the "professor," though there is no evidence he ever received a college degree.

GRANVILLE T. WOODS.

———————

Question #3: What was the Janney Coupler?" The Janney Coupler was invented by Eli H. Janney in 1873. It was used to connect railroad cars together. That coupler, however, led to the dangerous task of manually placing a pin in a link between the two cars, This led to accidents. Andrew Jackson Beard improved on the original design by making the coupling automatic. No one would lose a leg as Beard had in a coupling accident. His new coupler included two horizontal jaws, which automatically locked together upon joining. Recognizing Beard's safety improvement the US Congress passed the Federal Safety Appliance Act in 1887, which made it illegal to operate any railroad car without automatic couplers. That legacy was not bad for a guy born into slavery in Eastlake, Alabama. During his lifetime he patented a new double plow that permitted the distance between the two plow plates to be adjusted. He also patented a design for a new rotary steam engine. The man, it seemed, was always tinkering and inventing, gaining patents, and making a tidy sum in the process.

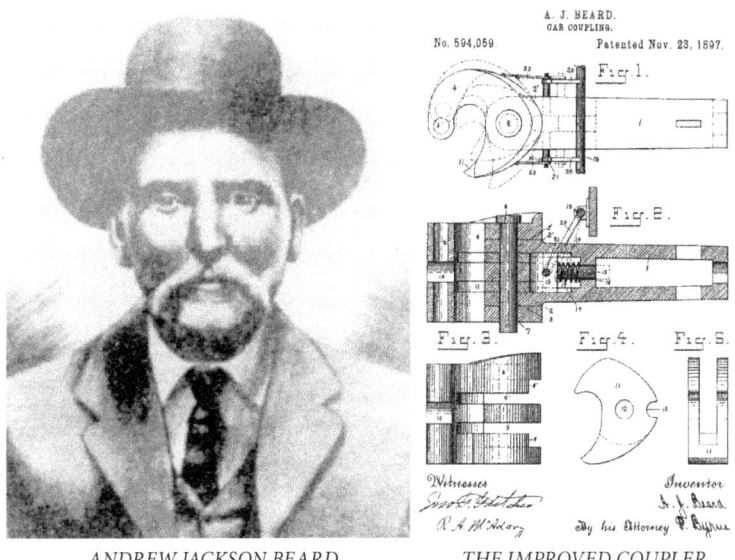

ANDREW JACKSON BEARD   THE IMPROVED COUPLER

––––––––––––––––––

Question #4 - What is a water closet? Strictly speaking, it is a toilet used on a railroad. The water closets used were known as a hopper toilet. At best it was some sort of flush system. At worse it was merely a hole in the floor. The major disadvantages of these methods were that it was (1) unhygienic and (2) dangerous to the environment. Waste material could and did drop onto the tracks, into rivers, and even at railroad stations. An air draft occurred when a flush toilet was used while the train was rolling along. This permitted dust and debris to rise up and assault the user. In 1874, Louis Howard Latimer described the need for his patented improved water closet as such: "The draft through the hopper being always excessive while the annoyance from dust, cinders, and other matters thrown up from the track is so great as to forbid or discourage the use of the apparatus except under extreme circumstances." Latimer was issued patent #147,363 on February 10, 1874. His toilet emptied through a trap door activated by the lid. His improved water closet made railroad travel both easier and safer.

145

LOUIS LATIMER

"I never knew…"

"Now you do, James."

"So many names…"

"And there are others, Rachel, who with sweat, muscle, and blood built the nation's railroads. In the South over 75% of the railways were built with slave labor before the Civil War."

"How did you learn about these people, Professor Jones?"

"Martha, I had to spend long hours looking at copious legal documents, newspaper accounts, personal letters and diaries. Plus, I interviewed as many folks as possible. Slowly, ever so slowly, a picture emerged, some of which I have shared with you today."

"There's still more?"

"There's always more, James and much for which we can be proud."

"Making the invisible visible?"

"A task that welcomes our youth."

DAY 4 – JULY 26, 1940

The Freeman family was huddled around the breakfast table. Tasty scrambled eggs and delightful pancakes had been eaten, along with crispy bacon. Sharp black coffee for the parents and hot chocolate for the children completed the early morning meal. Now it was time to plan the Fair visit for the day. As was his custom Mr. Freeman laid out maps and brochures on the kitchen table. As he did he said, "Today we visit the Government Zone and the Court of the States." All but one accepted his announcement.

"Dad…"
"James, the answer is no."
"But…"
"I talked it over with your mother and she held sway."
"Mom…"

James' sisters looked on with big smiles on their faces, as if to say, "Right on Mom and Dad."

"I'm old enough."
"Age is not the question."
"What is?"
"Sex."

————————

FAIR FACTS

It probably comes as a surprise that in the family-oriented New York World's Fair there were exhibitions of naked and near naked women. Of course, this was nothing new. All previous festivals in Europe and the United States had their fair share of burlesque and related girlie shows. By way of example… Little Egypt and other belly dancers were stars of the 1893 Chicago World's Fair. Peep shows were a staple of country fairs and carnivals all over the country. Men gravitated to these shows much like kids asking for cotton candy.

LITTLE EGYPT

A financial interest also was involved. The New York World's Fair desperately needed to rent out all of its concessions. Alluring female performances translated into more ticket sales. Historians of the Fair speak of the "deal with the devil." Exhibitors could only go so far and no further under the strict gaze of Mayor Fiorello LaGuardia. Two years before the Fair opened he had shut down New York's burlesque theatres. However, he now quietly relented for the good of the Fair. Kids couldn't attend a show, though many tried using any number of ruses. Patrons couldn't get too close to the women, especially those who were sunbathing in the nude in a public area. And most of all, the most alluring shows got going after most of the Fair closed down at 10:00pm. Still the Fair kept close eyes on things and if things went wrong…

MAYOR FIORELLO LAGUARDIA BUSTS THE NUDES

Some of the more interesting shows included Nils T. Granlund's *Congress of Beauty and Colony of Naked Sun Worshippers*. The ladies were all part of his burlesque revue. When not at work and merely sunning gawkers could get a clear view of the topless women. The onlookers were, however, fenced off from the gals. The old adage was in play: "look but don't touch."

GRANLUND'S LADIES

Salvador Dali prepared an exhibition called *Dali's Dream of Venus*. It was a surrealist funhouse designed by the artist himself. It was considered by many a "girlie show" since there were topless women in surreal tableaus. Others were floating in swimming pools or lying on a bed of lobsters. One was covered in body paint to look like a piano keyboard. With this in mind *Life Magazine* stated that one funhouse "stood out among the others." His exhibit was considered the "most amazing." Apparently even getting into the building was quite an experience for all patrons, men and women alike. Tickets cost $.25. You bought them at the fish-headed booth. As visitors passed through the entrance they were flanked by two towering legs clad in stockings and high-heels. Once inside there was a bit of conventional museum art. There were reproductions of Leonardo da Vinci's *John the Baptist* and Botticelli's *Birth of Venus*. They were viewed through openings in the irregular façade.

Once inside the building visitors entered a lavish grotto. A nude sleeping Venus reclined in a 36-foot long bed covered in white and red satin. Around and on her were flowers and leaves. Apparently she is dreaming. In the adjourning room there was an aquarium where women wore revealing costumes, which had fins and spikes. Some of the women tapped on giant typewriter keys or answered an oversized submerged telephone. It was all so surrealistic.

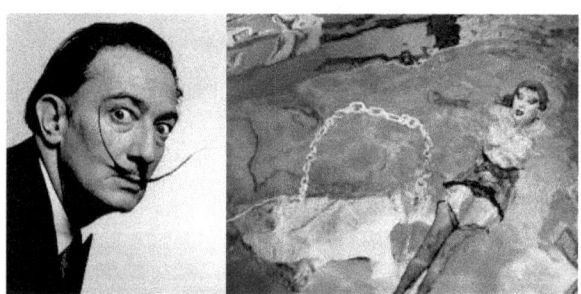

DALI'S FEMALE IN THE GHETTO

The most successful production at the Fair was *Billy Rose's Aquacade*. It took place in an Art Deco amphitheater that could seat 11,000 guests. The unique structure was located at the north end of Meadow Lake. Of course, there was a pool, almost Olympic-size for the aquatic events. There was also a 200-foot floating stage that was hidden behind a lighted 40-foot high curtain of water. The show had music, dance, and swimming. It featured two names known to an earlier generation: Johnny Weissmuller, an Olympian, and Eleanor Holm Jarret.

Another name was Busby Berkeley. He staged the aquatic performances that focused on family fare.

BILLY ROSE   THE AQUACADE SHOW

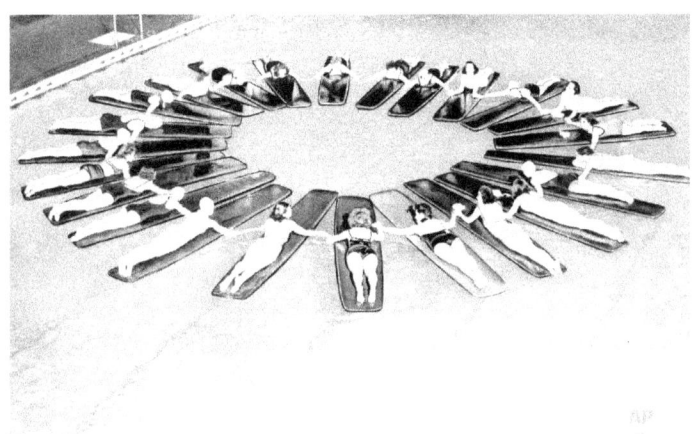

A BUSBY BERKELEY PRODUCTION

————————————

"Isn't a compromise possible, Dad?

"Meaning what, Rachel?"

"Just this. Martha and I would like to see the Billy Rose show. The performers are reasonably well covered, almost as if they were at Coney Island. We think Mom would also like to go? Right, Mom?"

"Yes, there's little that can harm James there."

"He could still fall for one of the shapely dancers."

For a moment all waited for the patriarch to say something; he did. "Okay, we'll see Billy Rose and his swimmers, but not Granlund's Ladies. That's too much even for me."

"Dad, what about Salvador Dali? It's pretty much all art."

"Rachel, I suspect you've talked with your mother?"

"You bet. She wants to see his off-the-wall stuff too. Don't worry about James. We'll sit on either side of him at the show and keep him out of trouble. Does that work for you? And don't forget, he's seen the cover of *Life Magazine* that reviewed the Fair."

"Do I have a choice?"

"Not if we vote."

Mr. Freeman, though always a "just in charge guy," was also exceedingly pragmatic. As he liked to say, "If you don't have the cards, walk away from the table."

"No need. I know when I'm licked. Now let's check out the map of the Government Zone."

"Rachel, which pavilion do you want to see?"

"The American Pavilion. I'm a stay at home gal."

"Martha?"

"The British pavilion."

"James?"

"The Russian exhibit."

"Really?"

"Yes."

"Dear?"

"The Japanese Pavilion. What about you?"

"The Jewish Palestine Pavilion."

"Is that a country?"

"Not yet, James."

"Okay, let's check the map again."

"Dad, we know where we're going."

"Rachel, it doesn't hurt to double check. We've got a lot on our agenda today."

That said, Mr. Freeman pulled out his now well-worn *Fair Guide* and checked the Government Zone map.

"On our way to the Jewish-Palestinian Pavilion in the Community of Interest Zone we'll pass by the Lagoon of the Nations and the Court of Nations. That's where they have the light show."

"We're coming back tonight to see the light show?"

"Yes, Martha. Your mother's heart is set on seeing it."

––––––––––––––––

FAIR FACTS

Combining lights and water the Lagoon of the Nations was one of the favorites of Fair visitors, so much so that critics said, "The show in the Lagoon gave the New York Fair it's most unique and perhaps it most artistically memorable element." Many claimed it was a new form of art. Once in operation the spectacular show was just that, really something to tell the folks back home. What most people didn't understand was how complicated and challenging it was to produce the show.

Here's how it worked. Over 1,000 water nozzles were needed to throw 20 tons of water into the air at a time. To do so some 400 jets were utilized, a well as an additional 350 firework jets. And on top of that about 3,000,000 watts of light were part of the display. Music was broadcasted in stereo to any number of speakers above and around the lagoon. Behind the scene three technicians controlled each night's display. They were located in the US Building. They sat at a console facing a massive number of switches and buttons that controlled everything much like a pilot in a cockpit. A "score" on paper instructed them as to what switches should be thrown or buttons pushed. The paper score was similar to the roll in a player piano. All this effort led to a fan favorite display of lights, water fountains, and music in front of the different foreign pavilions.

LAGOON OF THE NATIONS

————————————

"The Lagoon of the Nations is adjacent to the Court of Peace, isn't it, Dad?" James asked.

"Yes."

"But not by accident?"

"I think --- and this is only a guess --- the planners wanted the nations of the world to have a peaceful, tranquil area near their pavilions. When the Lagoon wasn't into its nightly extravaganza the waters were quiet, offering, I think, a place where diplomats could reflect on the weighty issues facing them. The Court of Peace, which was really nothing more than a physical location, symbolized the hope of most people that there were other ways of settling disputes short of armed conflict."

"If that's the case," Rachel interjected, "they need a Court of Peace in China, where the Japanese and the Chinese are locked in brutal combat."

"Why stop there?" Martha asked. "Hitler is threatening Poland after almost going to war with Czechoslovakia. If it wasn't for that paper signed in Munich, Europe would be at war now."

"That's a terrible thought, Martha. We can't go through that again. All those boys killed in the trenches, so horrible."

"Mother's right," Mr. Freeman added. "But I'm not sure we won't see war, not with Hitler running around in Berlin. He seems intent on aggression."

"FDR is trying to keep us neutral and out of any conflict," James said. "We've been talking about all this in class."

"What does your teacher think?"

"He thinks we better rearm and be prepared to fight all over the world. He doesn't like the draft but thinks the country has to expand its armed forces."

The word "draft" sounded like a bell in the night. The sisters looked at their brother, as did his parents. A clammy fear clouded their thoughts. James would soon be of draft age. Around them other visitors reflected on other things one assumes, the sights and sounds of a wonderful, sun-filled day at the Fair. As would be expected they were intent on having a good time, keeping at bay a terrible reality: Americans might be living in the twilight of peace.

James broke the spell, "I really enjoyed visiting the Temple of Religion yesterday."

"As did I, son. The concert we heard was really special. Imagine having an Aeolian-Skinner Pipe Organ and that 150-foot-high tower with stained glass windows."

"Mom, I heard there were almost 1,200 people in the auditorium."

THE TEMPLE OF RELIGION

FAIR FACTS

The Temple of Religion was designed to show America's fervent belief in the freedom of religion. The programs were all spiritual in nature but not sectarian. The themes were interdenominational, suggesting that all religions had something in common in a troubled world. This was done with pageants, concerts, and plays, plus lectures and discussions.

"We're Christians, aren't we, Mom?"

"So I've been told, James. What are you getting at?"

"With people believing in so many different things, I was wondering…"

"Yes?"

"Well, what's God's religion?"

Again, a question hung in the air. Mrs. Freeman did, however, have a ready answer.

"Maybe God's religion is in the Lagoon of Nations and in the Court of Peace. Maybe the answer is a world without war."

No one in the family disputed her remark.

CHAPTER 16 – PAVILIONS

Decisions had been made. The Freeman family knew what they planned to see. What they didn't know was the story behind the government pavilions.

FAIR FACTS

His name was Grover Whalen. Prior to his involvement with the New York World's Fair he was the police chief of the city. He was tough on crime, once saying, "There is plenty of law at the end of a night stick." Following that stint he enjoyed an unusual role in city politics. It was his job to welcome celebrities to New York, including royalty. He was the ideal person to be the "face of the city." He had social prominence, executive ability, and a warm personality in addition to being "well-connected, well-educated, and well off." He was a natural for an essential role if a world's fair was actually coming to New York. Someone had to travel the world and woo potential exhibitor nations, corporations, and individuals to participate. At this he was most successful, wooing 60 nations and 33 states and territories to join in the fun. Behind the scenes he played a major role in securing Flushing Meadows for the Fair's site.

GROVER WHALEN

Whalen accomplished all this within the "fair constraints" of his day. What did that mean? In 1928, twenty-one countries signed a treaty establishing the International Bureau of Expositions (IBE) to authorize and oversee future expositions. The treaty did not use the word "Fair." Europeans equated that term with a trade show, not an international exposition. The IBE required a formal request for authorization that had to be made in person. In addition, the host country's government had to accede to the request. In June 1937, the US House of Representatives passed a resolution authorizing the president to invite foreign powers to participate in the 1939 New York World's Fair. In November President Franklin D. Roosevelt issued a proclamation to that effect. Now it was up to Whalen to do his wooing.

He started quite unexpectedly with the Soviet Union. He traveled to Washington D.C. to meet with the acting Soviet ambassador to the United States. That was Konstantin Umansky. Whalen invited Russia to participate. This was a most unusual moment. A capitalist with strong ties to free enterprise and profitable companies was inviting a true-blue Communist and a devout Marxist to break bread in New York City. Surprising Whalen, the Soviet ambassador immediately placed a long distance call to the Kremlin and asked to speak with Joseph Stalin, the absolute ruler of Russia. As the story goes Stalin quickly mulled over the request and agreed to participate. Over $4,000,000 was set-aside for the Soviet Pavilion. The Russian bear was coming to the Big Apple. Stalin's motivations are difficult to discern. Perhaps it was simply a matter of national pride. The Kremlin would showcase Russia's success under Communist rule. Another possibility was that Stalin wanted to improve relations with Western Europe given the rise of Nazi Germany. Regardless, Whalen used this success story to garner agreements from other European nations.

––––––––––––

"Did you believe the size of that pavilion?" Mr. Freeman asked with a heightened degree of patriotic fervor.

"Dad, it was big enough to hold two venues: the main Soviet Pavilion and the Soviet Arctic Pavilion."

"And what about the statue of the worker on top of the Main Pavilion," Rachel said. "It was the second tallest building at the Fair after the Trylon."

"But that caused a fuss, didn't it, Dad?"

"It sure did. It was higher than the flag on the American Pavilion."

"People were upset that it was even higher than the statue of George Washington, to whom the Fair was dedicated."

"Again, you're right, Rachel."

"They sure pushed Stalin," Martha said. "That relief of him on the façade of the building was impressive."

"It seemed like there was a lot of propaganda in this venue."

"Where did you get that thought, James?"

"My history teacher told me to watch out for it. Mr. Bechtel was quite vigorous about that when he heard I would visit."

FAIR FACTS

The Soviet Union wasted no time or money in its propagandistic messages. They were everywhere. The gigantic and monumental architecture... The use of expensive construction materials like marble and precious stones... And in commentary... The USSR claimed it was a country that:

...ended exploitation of men by men, eliminated racial and national animosities and in which 170,000,000 people of different nationalities are united in a voluntary, equal federation of eleven socialist Republics.

The propaganda efforts took an unusual tact. Where America's theme was the *World of Tomorrow* represented by innovative projects in engineering, technology, and science influencing every aspect of American life, the Russian propaganda claimed they had already achieved the "world of tomorrow." Simply put, America was envisioning a future that the Soviets believed was already present. The Russian venue included models of newly built factories, electric stations, and dioramas and graphics illustrating railways, ships, and airplanes. By contrast, they didn't exhibit the wonders of television, new automobile models, or the latest commercial wares of every possible type. That was to be expected; the Soviets were proclaiming the virtues of non-competitive, less commercialized society unlike America's consumption of the latest you-know-what. In some ways the New York World's Fair had become a proxy struggle between two economic models, socialism versus capitalism, the collective versus the individual, and authoritarian government versus the democratic process. The Fair had become a battleground of ideas.

In one area in particular the Soviets had made their mark. The Arctic was the last "blank space" on the map. In the 1930's the Russians conquered it. Russia was the first country to successfully land an airplane on ice. It was first to make a nonstop transpolar flight from Moscow to Vancouver and then to California. That was in 1937. The long-range plane used was the ANT-25. It was placed at the front of the Soviet Pavilion, where it demonstrated the "inextricable connection" between the Arctic and aviation in the USSR.

THE RUSSIAN ANT-25

At the same time Russia established a scientific station on a drifting slab of ice. In 1939 the famous icebreaker, the *Joseph Stalin*, was the first ship to reach the North Pole. All this the Soviets showcased in the Arctic portion of their pavilion. It told the story of the "modern epic of exploration and pioneering." The victorious conquest of the Arctic impressed American visitors. Paradoxically, in the Arctic the Russians were kin to the Fair's vision: *The World of Tomorrow*.

Soviet explorers, scientists, seamen, aviators and workers have converted the Arctic into a navigable seaway, and are making immense areas within the Arctic Circle habitable.

———————————

"Well, James, what do you think?"

"Dad, I loved the aviation bit. I really wanted to jump into the ANT-25. Think of it… Flying so far, from one continent to another, nonstop over ice and oceans. What an adventure that would be."

"James sounds like a Russian paid spokesperson," Rachel said with a charming smile.

"Or at least like a guy who should enlist in the Army Air Force," Martha quickly added.

That simple statement quieted the family. It took Martha a moment to realize what happened. There were no Black pilots in the Army or the Navy. There were no Black pilots flying commercial airlines. There were only a handful of Blacks with a license to fly a small private airplane. Much like professional baseball and football Blacks were excluded. James' youthful ambitions to fly would not easily be realized.

———————

As they left the Soviet Pavilion Rachel said, "I wonder if we would be better off in the Soviet Union? They say all people are treated equally. That would apply to us too, wouldn't it?"

"That's what they say, Rachel, but I don't know."

"Dad, we say it too but…"

"That's true, we do."

"Well, then?"

"Rachel, things are not perfect here. No doubt about that, but things are better than before. For right now I go with FDR, not Stalin, no matter what the Russians say. Anyway, this is our home. Even if others dispute it we're as American as anyone. We're tied to its past and bound to its future. Now it's time to visit our British cousins."

———————

"There it is," Martha said in an unusually high-pitched voice. "The two police officers ahead of us are holding it. Let's get closer."

Joined by others the Freeman family inched closer to the two British constables holding a shatter proof glass container containing the holiest of holies in the history of the United Kingdom. The officers were standing in front of the entrance to the British Pavilion providing visitors with a momentary peek at the *Great Charter*, often referred to as the *Magna Carta*. Of course, as Martha had told her family the document held by the officers was only a replica of the *Magna Carta Liberatum* (Latin for Great Charter of Freedoms). The actual copy was on the first floor of the British Pavilion protected behind a bulletproof casing with two officers always on duty. Still, it was fun to glimpse the facsimile and pretend it was the real thing.

As the family walked toward the Main Building, Mr. Freeman said, "Martha, how do you know all this?"

"Dad, I took a class in English history last semester. That's when we learned about poor King John."

"King John?"

"He was pushed by the barons sign a royal document drafted by the Archbishop of Canterbury to conclude a peace between the unpopular king and a group of rebellious barons. The Archbishop was Stephen Langton. The agreement, sometimes referred to as the *Royal Charter*, was signed near Windsor at a spot called Runnymede. The date was June 15, 1215."

"What did the agreement say?" Rachel asked.

"It promised the protection of church rights in addition to protecting the barons from illegal imprisonment. It promised access to swift justice and limitations on feudal payments to the Crown. If I recalled correctly a council of 25 barons would implement the agreement. All this was stipulated in Latin. My professor showed us a copy of the agreement which, of course, no one in the class could read, not even a couple of Catholic students. Taking mercy on us he showed us a cartoon drawing that cleared up everything in an amusing way."

"He also pointed out that the *Charter* was an essential foundation of Britain's unwritten constitution and a controlling influence on Parliament's powers. The 'divine right of kings' was cast off, as well as the arbitrary edicts of a Prime Minister in favor of personal liberties."

———————

"Look at all the flags on the building," Mrs. Freeman remarked. "It looks like the entire British Empire is here."

"Mom, it should. The British Pavilion includes Australia, New Zealand and the British Colonial Empire, including East Africa, West Africa, the West Indies, and the Far East. The Canadians have their own separate pavilion proclaiming, I think, a degree of independence within the Commonwealth."

THE BRITISH PAVILION

Along with many others the Freemans moved into the Main Building, and following a flood of visitors went into the room that housed the *Magna Carta*. Without question the document was the main attraction and the British knew it. That's why they brought it to the Fair. To protect it, as noted earlier, two security guards were on duty at all times. This was no idle concern. Earlier in the Fair a time bomb, disguised as a portable radio, was discovered in the British Pavilion on July 4, 1940. The bomb was removed to an open field on the fairgrounds. Unfortunately it detonated, killing two detectives assigned to disarming it. With an empire stretching around the world the British had made both friends and foes. That being the case heightened security was a necessity.

THE DISPLAY ROOM

————————————

"Martha, didn't the *Magna Carta* influence the early American colonists and the call for a revolution?"

"It did, James. Colonials wanted the same rights of Englishmen living in Britain, rights which they felt were abrogated in the colonies."

"Abrogated?"

"Ended or denied."

"It influenced our Declaration of Independence?"

"Indeed."

"And the Bill of Rights?"

"Yes."

"Then I have a question."

At that moment Mr. Freeman jumped into the conversation, "Watch out, Martha. The provocateur is circling."

"Provocateur?"

"What your father means, James, is an inquisitive young man who provokes a little with his questions." This James' mother pointed out with half-a-smile.

"Well then, what is your question, dear brother?"

"The agreement of 1215 protected the barons, right?"

"Right?"

"What about the common people?"

"In time. It took what the British call the Glorious Revolution of 1688 to expand what we would call civil liberties to those beyond royal families and titled individuals."

"Much like our Constitution?"

"What are you getting at, James?"

"Weren't the framers of the Constitution landowners, bankers, and business people?"

"Meaning?"

"Well, weren't they like the barons? Were they making sure their interests were protected?

"Well, yes."

"And didn't that include slave owners?"

"Yes."

Mr. Freeman saw where this was going. Visiting the New York World's Fair had somehow kindled in James a lurking desire to understand the place of Blacks in American society. What James said next did not surprise him.

"It seems like the average person in Britain, as well as in our country were something of an after thought, the wealthy and powerful first and only later were rights expanded."

"Martha, James has a good point," Mrs. Freeman said. "Progress, especially for our people has been slow and not always without difficulty and pain. But the line of history is upward, isn't that what you're getting at James?"

"Yes, I think so."

FAIR FACTS

The attempt to explode a bomb at the British Pavilion on July 4, 1940 has an unusual history. A switchboard operator received an anonymous call "saying that there was a bomb planted in the British exhibit." The caller stated the bomb would soon go off and visitors should leave the area. The exact words were, "Get out!" A short time later an electrician discovered a suspicious satchel in the ventilation room in an upper level of the packed British Pavilion. Patrol officers on duty gingerly removed the case to a remote area behind the Polish Pavilion. There they waited for the bomb squad. Two officers arrived on the scene, Ferdinand Socha and Joseph J. Lynch. They checked the satchel. It was ticking. The bomb squad in those days did not have much in the way of protective clothing or safety equipment. The two officers were dressed in their regular clothes. They only had simple tools to work with and relatively little experience. Using a pocketknife they cut a small hole in the case. They knew immediately it was the real thing. Those were their last thoughts. The bomb went off killing both men. Other officers nearby were wounded from shrapnel fragments. Later it was estimated that the bomb had the equivalent of 12 sticks of dynamite. The resulting blast created a hole in the ground five feet wide and three feet deep. Though an investigation was immediate and thorough no one was ever arrested. The blast continued to be a mystery over the years.

By EDWARD DILLON and GERALD DUNCAN.

A dynamite bomb, plucked from the midst of throngs in the British Pavilion, exploded at 5:20 P. M. yesterday in the World's Fair grounds while 168,000 visitors roamed the exposition. Two detectives, examining a suitcase containing the deadly explosive, were killed instantly. Five other police were injured, two of them critically.

Thousands of holiday-makers were near by when the bomb, apparently planted by enemies of Great Britain, blew up with a roar like a cannon on a grassy plot be-

Photodiagram of the route over which the bomb was carried will be found on page 20.

hind the Polish Building, opposite the Gardens on Parade. Hats, strips of clothing, shoes and fragments of bodies were hurled through the air over a 50-foot radius as the explosion tore a ½-foot crater in the ground. Many thought the explosion was part of the Fourth of July celebration. Within a few moments 10,000 sightseers crowded

Killed in Fair Explosion

The late Ferdinand Socha
The late Joseph J. Lynch
Met instant death in holiday tragedy.

During the New York World's Fair Germany attacked Poland. This action ignited the Second World War on the European continent. The actual copy of the *Magna Carta* exhibited could not be returned to Britain due to wartime conditions. The copy was sent to Fort Knox, Kentucky for safekeeping. It was placed in a secure vault during the war. It would be returned to Britain when the war ended. While at Fort Knox the document was in good company. The original Constitution and the Declaration of Independence were also stored at Fort Knox. The two documents were kept under lock and key. They were sealed with lead and then placed in an additional protective container weighing close to 150 pounds.

The New York Times.

EXTRA

GERMAN ARMY ATTACKS POLAND;
CITIES BOMBED, PORT BLOCKADED;
DANZIG IS ACCEPTED INTO REICH

NY TIMES, SEPTEMBER 1, 1939

CHAPTER 17 – THE TEA GARDEN

Mrs. Freeman had any number of reasons to feel good today beginning with her desire to visit the Japanese Pavilion and, if possible, participate in a tea ceremony. She had always been fascinated by the Far East. The enjoyable cause of this disposition lurked in her past, when she attended Howard University in Washington D.C. Professor Lawrence, a skinny twig of a man but with a vast knowledge of Japanese and Chinese history, had kept his students (or at least her) spellbound as he took the class through 3,000 years of Asian history. Though she was a devout Christian and accepted Jesus as her savior she still found herself lured by Zen Buddhism and Shintoism. Her faith in the Gospels did not suffer, nor did her steadfast belief in the messages of Old Testament prophets, particularly the words of Amos.

But let justice roll down like waters and righteousness like an ever-flowing stream. (Amos 5-24)

She also found the Psalms inspiring as she did Isaiah's mandate.

Give justice to the weak and the fatherless: maintain the right of the afflicted and the destitute. (Psalm 82.3)

Learn to do good; seek justice, and correct oppression, bring justice to the fatherless, and please the widow's cause. (Isaiah 1:17)

The notion of justice was close to her heart and one she had inculcated into her children. "Always," she told them, "seek social justice and promote fairness, and be kind in your judgment of others." The older daughters accepted this admonition and practiced it in their lives. And now young James, by virtue of his inquisitiveness, was moving quickly in that direction.

Mrs. Freeman had another reason to be happy today. In a few minutes she would meet Augusta Savage, who had promised to share her artistic thoughts about the Shinto Temple the family was about to see.

JAPANESE PAVILION

FAIR FACTS

Yasuo Matsui designed the Japanese Pavilion. Curiously, he was a Japanese-American architect. The complex was designed to look like a traditional Shinto Shrine set within a Japanese Garden. The interior had a number of rooms. In a time of on-going Japanese incursions into China and uneasy relations with the United States, it was appropriate that one room was called the "Diplomat Room." The room featured a replica of the Liberty Bell. It was made out of pearls and diamonds, valued at close to a million dollars. The room also had a mural on which was written: *Dedicated to Eternal Peace and Friendship between America and Japan.*

THE DIPLOMAT ROOM

The friendship theme began with the "Flame of Friendship" that was lighted in Japan at the Grand Shrine at Izumo. It then traveled almost 11,000 miles to reach New York. Kimono-clad Japanese girls in wooden-soiled sandals accompanied the "sacred flame." The girls were always smiling and charming.

———————

"Augusta, at last. We've missed you."
"As I have you, Mrs. Freeman."

The family traded hugs all around. Even a somewhat timid James got into the spirit of things. Mr. Freeman, as always, had a paternalistic smile for all.

"Shall we go in?"

Along with many others our little group walked into the Japanese Pavilion, which meant they entered a large imposing room. It was called the "Silk Room." Two beautiful Japanese women, each dressed in traditional silk kimonos, were in the room. The room furnishings straddled two cultures, Western style furniture but Eastern style fabric. There seemed to be a fair balance uniting two cultures across the vast Pacific.

MODEL SILK ROOM, JAPAN PAVILION

They next moved into the Tea Room. There a young woman explained that the tea ceremony actually originated in China and was raised to an art form in Japan. The ceremony begins by preparing tea for an honored guest. The ceremony is called "chado or sado." That translates as "hot water tea." A series of intricate movements is performed in a strict order established over hundreds of years. Food is served with the tea: soup, rice, and seasoned food such as raw fish. The food is served on a large square wooden tray. The tea is served in the same cup for all guests. Each person is encouraged (or knows by tradition) to turn the cup slightly before sipping.

Of course, when visitors were asked to participate in the ceremony the Freeman ladies jumped at the chance. They quickly lapsed into the spirit of the tea ceremony much to the joy of their Japanese hosts. When the ceremony was over the family moved on to the Japanese gardens. To do so, they had to pass through a most beautiful room in the interior of the pavilion. It was there that Augusta Savage held sway.

THE INTERIOR ROOM   THE JAPANESE GARDEN

"You understand I'm not an expert on Oriental gardens, but I do have some acquaintance with the topic. Almost always you will find a strong use of rocks or stone to form the structure of the landscape. Water is, of course, important. It represents life-giving forces, not only for humans but also the plants that provide color and symbolize the change in seasons. The most common flowers are azaleas, magnolias, camellias, and dwarf trees. If the climate cooperates flowering cherry trees add a most memorable look to the garden. Overall, the landscape is designed as a peaceful, natural space to detach oneself from the hectic pace of life that defines our everyday world. It is a place to achieve calmness, even to meditate, but always to regain your sense of being, what many simply call your 'balance.' Some gardens include a small bridge edging over a pond."

"Augusta, I could stay here the whole day. It is such a peaceful place."

"It is."

"It's too bad we can't take it home to Harlem and elsewhere."

"Oh, but we can in our hearts and memories, and, if you choose to do so, you can adorn your backyard with stones and flowers, and perhaps even a little shelter, there to create your own place of peace."

Listening to all this Mr. Freeman gave into the inevitable. He would take another look at the overgrown plants and scrubs in his tiny yard. That, he knew, would make his wife most happy. And perhaps there he would find some peace from the disturbing racial issues that shadowed Blacks even in Harlem.

As they were leaving the Japanese Pavilion our little group came across children gazing at Japanese dolls. As it turns out they were for sale in the local gift shop. But not only dolls… Tea sets made in Japan were also for sale. Mrs. Freeman pointed this out to her husband. Taking stock of the situation he grasped the initiative, saying, "Dear, wouldn't it be nice to have a tea set?"

JAPANESE DOLLS AND A TEA SET

CHAPTER 18 – THE JEWISH PALESTINE PAVILION

"Dad, I don't get it. Jewish Palestine isn't a country."

"So, James?"

"Well, how can it have a pavilion?"

Mr. Freeman took a moment before answering. He needed to get things straight in his own mind. Just why was he prodding his family to visit a pavilion honoring a country that didn't exist? How would he explain why the New York World's Fair agreed to permit this pavilion for an area of British military and civilian control in the Middle East? Would he divulge his own personal feelings for visiting this pavilion? These questions he considered before answering his son.

"James, before I answer your questions take a look at the Jewish Palestine Building, especially the three statues in front of us."

"You're looking at three 14-foot hammered copper relief figures."

"They sure dominate the exterior wall," Martha said. "I wonder what do they symbolize?"

"I know," Rachel quickly said. "The one on the left is called *The Toiler of the Soil*. The middle figure is *The Laborer*. The right hand figure is *The Scholar*."

THE RELIEF FIGURES

"And how do you know all this?" Mrs. Freeman asked.

"We learned about this in my Art Appreciation class this semester and the man behind the work."

"Who was?" Mr. Freeman asked.

"Maurice Ascalon. He's sometimes called the 'father of modern Israeli decorative arts.'"

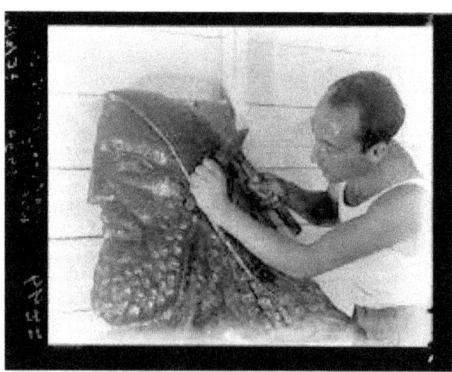

CREATING THE IMAGES

"What can you tell us about the images, Rachel?"

"What I learned was this. The images extol hard work and scholarship, physical labor and intellectual pursuits. According to my professor labor was needed to reclaim the land from swamps... To bring irrigation to the desert wastes... To cultivate the land to feed a people..."

"Okay, I get it. Hard work... Okay... But what's with the name? Is this a Jewish pavilion? Is it a Palestinian pavilion? I don't get it. Dad?"

"I've read a few things. This is what I know."

––––––––––––

FAIR FACTS

The organizers of the Fair had a problem. Jews in Palestine had requested participation in the New York World's Fair. A Jewish Palestine pavilion made sense. The largest concentration of Jews in the United States was in the New York metropolitan area. American Jews supported the idea of space in the international zone for an exhibit. The strict Fair guidelines, however, only recognized established countries. There was no Jewish state. There was no Arab-Palestinian state. There were only two groups, one prompted by Zionism, the other pushed by Arab nationalism, each seeking a national homeland and recognition as a nation. Given that, the application for space was rejected. There was immediate pushback and eventually a compromise was reached. Jewish Palestine would be granted a spot under the "broad spectrum of Great Britain" due to the League of Nations mandate held by the British. Jewish Palestine would be granted exhibition space in the Community Interest Zone. Accepting the application did not amount to recognizing either a Jewish or Arab state.

––––––––––––

"Mandate? What's that?" James asked.

That, as it turned out, was Martha's cue.

"In my Modern European history class we learned about the 'mandate system.' In the aftermath of the Great War, decisions were made in Paris to breakup the Ottoman Empire in the Middle East and German possessions in Africa and in the Pacific. This was part of what was called the Treaty of Versailles. With the agreement of the United States 'spoils of war' were divided up among France, Britain, and Japan.

This process took place under what was called the Mandate System. Specific countries had a mandate to govern these possessions until such time they could be granted their interdependence."

"What did this have to do with Jewish Palestine?"

"It all begins with a British Foreign Secretary."

FAIR FACTS

Arthur Balfour was the British Foreign Secretary in the years following the Great War. He was deeply involved in Britain's mandate in the Middle East that included Palestine and Trans-Jordan. Pressured by many Jewish organizations, Balfour sent a letter to Baron Walter Rothschild, a major leader of the British Jewish community. In this correspondence he expressed the government's interest in establishing a Jewish homeland in Palestine. This statement came to be known as the Balfour Declaration. At the time Jews only accounted for 11% of the population in Palestine. Arab Christians accounted for 9.5%. Arabs accounted for an overwhelming percentage of the inhabitants. That being the case there was understandable Arab resistance to a future Jewish State, since such an entity would be carved out of land historically under Arab influence. This resistance increased as over 100,000 Jews migrated to Palestine in the 1920's. The rise of Hitler Germany and Nazi policies toward Jews accelerated this movement. By the late 1930's Palestine was a 'tinderbox' of competing territorial claims and increasing conflict between Jews and Arabs. Inevitably, British troops attempting to keep the peace found themselves caught in the middle.

BALFOUR AND THE BRITISH MANDATE

"Martha, I assume you got an A in the class."

"I did, Mom."

"Let's get back to the pavilion," James said in a strong voice. "The Fair Committee approved the request for space. I get that. What happened next?"

"I'll answer that," Mr. Freeman quickly responded. "Here I know a few things of interest. A significant fundraising drive took place to provide the 'gelt' for the pavilion."

"Gelt?"

"James, the Yiddish or Hebrew word for gold. I think the term originated with the Germans or the Dutch. In any event, money was raised no thanks to the leadership of Thomas Mann, a Nobel Prize winner and a German refugee. The cornerstone for the pavilion was dedicated on May 13, 1939. Hanita provided the cornerstone."

"Hanita?"

"It was the most recent Jewish settlement just west of Galilee deep within Arab-controlled territory. The first structures built were the 'tower and stockade.' In a way this settlement reminded many of American log forts along the trails leading west to Oregon and California."

THE TOWER UNDER CONSTRUCTION

In any event the Jewish Palestine Pavilion opened to the public on May 13, 1939. Mayor LaGuardia welcomed the first visitors with a smile and a quiet reminder:

"...the exhibit had special significance at this time, when the problem of a refuge for Jews persecuted by the totalitarian governments is growing more acute from day to day."

––––––––––––––––

LATER

"That was most interesting," Rachel said. "The exhibition hall really highlighted the history of Jews in Palestine and how they've turned barren land into a fertile landscape."

"A real land of 'milk and honey.'" Mrs. Freeman added. "They're making the desert bloom."

"What about the eternal light?" Martha asked. "What did they call it?"

"Ner Ha-Tamid," James said. "It is a lamp that burns perpetually in a Jewish Synagogue, either before or near the sacred scriptures of the law. I think they call that the Torah. The light is never allowed to go out. Oil lamps are still used in some synagogues, but electric lights can also be used."

"James, how did you know that?"

"Mom, I read the leaflet they handed out."

"James, do you know the story about how the eternal light got to New York? I hear it came from Palestine. Is that right?"

"Right on, Martha. Let me see if I can remember what the Rabbi told me when I was looking at the 'eternal light.' The date was April 9, 1938. The place was the historic 'Wailing Wall' in Jerusalem. The 'flame' was in a bronze oil lamp. It was given to Mrs. Ellen Yaardi. She boarded a Cunard White Star liner, the *Aquitania*. The ship reached New York harbor a few weeks later. The flame was immediately placed prominently in the pavilion's Memorial Hall."

"You remembered all that?"

"I guess so, Mom."

Perhaps it was sibling rivalry or just competitive juices... No matter what, Rachel couldn't resist the urge to one up her brother.

"Okay, James, tell me about the certificate?"

"What certificate?"

"The one we bought."

"What are you talking about?"

––––––––––––

To raise funds for the pavilion certificates were sold for $.25. It entitled the holder to one preferred admission to "The Holy Land of Yesterday and Tomorrow" at the Jewish Palestine Pavilion. That would have meant $1.25 for the Freeman family who were already on a tight budget. The certificate referred to the Jewish quarter in Palestine as the "Land of Israel," suggesting that this would be the name of a future Jewish State.

"Dad, you're being very quiet. What gives?"
"Rachel, I was just thinking."
"That was obvious."
"Well, perhaps what I'm about to say isn't so obvious."

Mr. Freeman's remark got the attention of everyone, as did the seriousness that clouded his face.

"I think we're like the Jews."

Mr. Freeman statement came right out of the blue. Not to make too fine a point, his words caught everyone off guard.

"The Jews are a distinct group. Not by color or race as much as by culture. Too often they've experienced prejudice and discrimination, and outright violence. We see all of that in Germany today with the Nazi regime picking on a small, almost defenseless group. Their businesses are being shut down. Their kids can't go to school. They're being removed from better housing, and in the middle of the night some are disappearing. Well, what does all of this remind you of? The question is not that hard. Isn't that what's happening to Blacks in the Jim Crow South? All that Plessy vs. Ferguson stuff about 'separate but equal,' leading to what? I'll tell you... Second class citizenship backed up by fear and lynch-violence, and all those damn bombings of Black churches and schools, all just like the Jews in Hitler's vision of a master race. Well, we've been through that during slave days. The white overseers were our masters. They separated our kids from their parents. They sold us like a commodity, human flesh for profit. They kept us from learning to read and write. They took away our dignity. In many ways we're mirror images of the Jews. They want a homeland to be safe. They want a place where they can worship without fear. They want to give their children hope. They want everything we want. They're going to have to fight for it with a sea of Arabs opposed to nationhood. Jews from all over the world will endure this fight. What about us? We're not going back to Africa no matter the urging of Marcus Garvey. We're staying here. This is our homeland. We're Black Jews in America."

Mr. Freeman's pent up tirade slowed and ended. The anger of his words dissipated but not their meaning. He was tired of it all. He wanted an "eternal light" of his own... For his family... For his people...

Mr. Freeman was, of course, unaware of Albert Einstein's comments about the Jewish situation in Palestine, which in many ways mirrored the Black's place in American society.

Remember, however, that in the life of a people and especially in times of need, there can be only one source of security, namely confidence in one's own strength and steadfastness. There could be no greater calamity than a permanent discord between us and the Arab people.

CHAPTER 19 – THE STATES

DAY 5 – JULY 27, 1940

The Freeman family was resting. It had been a long day visiting five state pavilions, threading their way through thick crowds, and enduring the humid New York weather. Because of the many venues involved the family had parceled out its energies on an individual basis. Each member would go to a different pavilion. By the end of the day the family would have visited the Pennsylvania Pavilion adjacent to the Lagoon, and not far from the Nevada exhibit. Members of the family would also visit the Georgia and Illinois Pavilions, as well as the Texas Pavilion. Afterwards they would all meet for a mid-day meal at the Turf Trylon Café in the Communication Zone. The Café could seat 1,000 people in addition to an outdoor mezzanine and two terraces, one on the balcony and the other in a beautiful garden, where the prices were a bit more modest. That's where the Freemans would rest their weary limbs. That's where the family was now. Everyone had ordered the complete dinner. Whether it was beef, chicken, or fish, the costs was the same: $1.25 per meal, including New York's best water or Columbia's best coffee. It should be noted that Mr. Freeman ordered a Budweiser beer --- $.10. It was a well-deserved expenditure given his efforts to prod the family to share individual experiences.

THE FREEMAN FAMILY TREK

THE TURF TRYLON CAFÉ

FAIR FACTS

The Court of States was an immediate hit with Fair visitors. In all, 23 states participated in the Fair. All but two state pavilions were grouped near the Lagoon of Nations and the United States Building. The two exceptions were Florida and New York. They were located near Fountain Lake in the Amusement Zone. Though not a state, Puerto Rico participated and was with the larger group. The Fairs National Board of Design permitted the states to use traditional designs to reflect their individual state themes. By contrast individual nations were required to have original architecture. All the state pavilions reflected the Fair's theme that this was "everyman's fair."

The Fair showed the way toward the improvement of all factors contributing to human welfare. We are convinced that the potential assets, material and spiritual of our country, are such that if rightly used they will make for a general public good such as has never before been known.

And continuing:

In order to make its contribution toward this process the Fair will show the most promising developments of production, service, and social factors of the present day in relation to their bearing on the life of the great mass of people.

ENTRANCE TO THE COURT OF STATES

————————————

Refreshed by their meal and a hefty slice of apple pie the family mulled over the day's events. Mrs. Freeman was first to share.

Mrs. Freeman

"I really enjoyed the Pennsylvania Pavilion. Wasn't it marvelous how they created an exact replica of Philadelphia's Independence Hall? You would have thought you were in the city of 'brotherly love.' But not only that… That oversized copy of the Liberty Bell was something. I really needed my reading glasses for the myriad of historical documents that were on display."

"Not always brotherly love for Blacks!"

"James, enough. We all know what took place."

"Mom's right, James. Let's just enjoy the day. Tomorrow will take care of itself, I think."

"Dad…"

Mr. Freeman didn't respond to his son's salutation. He just gave the young man his best "knock it off" look. It worked this time.

INDEPENDENCE HALL AT THE FAIR

Rachel

Rachel was up next, pointing out how much she enjoyed the Texas Pavilion. "I don't know how they did it but creating the façade of the Texas Building to look like the Alamo, well that was something. You would have thought you were there with Jim Bowie, Davy Crockett, and all those guys. And once I was inside that air-conditioned auditorium and out of the humanity that was heaven. I liked the large-scale relief map of Texas and all the realistic miniature figures on it involved with the Spanish missions and the battles of the Alamo and San Jacinto. I learned a great deal about the city of Austin, the state's capital, the cattle drives, and the discovery of oil."

THE FAÇADE   *THE BATTLE OF THE ALAMO*

"I have a question?"

"James?"

"Wasn't that battle just a land grab? All those people flooding into Texas from the East who didn't want to live under Mexico City's control. And didn't some of those people want to extend slavery into the area? And didn't a lot of people just resent pledging allegiance to Mexico and promising to be good Catholics? And..."

This time it was Mrs. Freeman who cut off James, though secretly she admired his questioning mind.

"James, there is much to what you say. That cannot be denied but this isn't the time. Okay? Now who is up next, James?"

"I am."

"James, be kind on our ears."

"Mom, I really got into the Nevada exhibit that wasn't there."

"The dam?"

"Yeah, I really wanted to see it."

———————

FAIR FACTS

Nevada was a young state. It wanted and needed an influx of residents. To that end it dangled some financial lures at the Fair such as not having a state income tax or an inheritance tax. But for most visitors to the pavilion the real attraction was the large replica of Boulder Dam (or Hoover Dam if you prefer).

BOULDER DAM

In 1928, the Republican-controlled Congress authorized the construction of an arch-gravity dam in the Black Canyon of the Colorado River on the border between Arizona and Nevada. The future dam, it was hoped, would provide hydroelectric power for the Southwest and California on the coast. The dam would also control floods and benefit farmers with irrigation water, permitting a semi-arid region to prosper as it helped to feed the nation. It took four years to construct the beautiful curved dam (1931-1935). Work began under President Herbert Hoover and ended during the administration of Franklin D. Roosevelt. It was dedicated on September 30, 1935. The creation of the dam led to holding back an almost unlimited amount of water, creating a manmade reservoir that was called Lake Mead.

Building the dam took a massive effort. Thousands of men worked around the clock to harness the Colorado River. Though great machines were used to build the concrete marvel it was still a backbreaking ordeal, if not a dangerous enterprise. Over 100 men died over four years. The numbers involved are almost beyond imagination. First, the dam cost $49 million dollars. That would be $713 million dollars today. Tax dollars were used for the project. The dam is 726 feet high and 1,044 feet long. It contains 4,400,000 cubic yards of concrete. Four giant reinforced concrete intake towers located above the dam divert water from the reservoir (Lake Mead) into huge steel pipes. Water in the pipes falls 500 feet to a hydroelectric plant at the base of the dam, where it turns 176 huge vertical hydroelectric turbines, which rotate a series of electric generators that make electric power. Nearly half of the power created keeps the lights on in Southern California.

James

"All right, James, so what happened to the dam exhibit? That's what we want to know."

"Mom, I asked a lot of questions. This is what I know. The Nevada State Highway Department was in charge of bringing the replica dam to New York. It was quite an undertaking. The Highway Department would then assemble the dam and be in charge of showing how everything worked. This was a real, large-scale working model."

"So what happened?" Martha asked.

"Unions..."

"What?"

"The unions wanted to be in charge. They had an exclusive contract with the New York World's Fair Committee to set up and run exhibits where their skills were required. For example, the union wanted fulltime electrical workers to operate the dam's mechanism and be present at all times during the Fair. Other unions also made their demands. All this drove up the cost of the exhibit. The Fair Committee admitted they couldn't guarantee the Nevada exhibit wouldn't be sabotaged if Nevada refused to pay the union's excessively high labor charges. In the end

Nevada wouldn't comply. The replica dam materials were packed up and shipped back west."

"That's quite a story, James."

"Martha, I really wanted to see how the dam worked."

At this point Mr. Freeman looked to the future, saying to his son, "One of these days you'll travel to Nevada and see the real dam at work. Just keep that in the back of your mind, James."

It was at this point that Rachel interjected a throwaway question.

"James, exactly what's the name of this dam? Is it the Boulder Dam or the Hoover Dam?"

"Initially the project was called the Hoover Dam in the 1920's. Then the Roosevelt Administration changed the name to the Boulder Dam in the 1930's. When the Republicans regain control of the Congress the name will probably be changed again. I guess that's politics."

"One last question, dear brother. Who owns the dam?"

James smiled in a teasing way before saying, "We do."

"What?"

"The American taxpayers paid for it. The federal government owns and operates the dam for us. Pretty cool, uh?"

Martha

It was now Martha's turn to share her thoughts about the Georgia Pavilion and its unique place in colonial America.

"The exhibit was very nice and informative, especially about colonial architecture in the Deep South. This was particularly true of the Georgia State Building housing the state's exhibits. Learning about the music and folklore of the state was fine. What really intrigued me was the story of the Georgia colony and an English philanthropist named Sir James Oglethorpe. He envisioned a refuge for his fellow man miles away from the poverty of London and the imprisonment of debtors. He looked to the New World and Britain's colonization of North America.

There he hoped to establish a colony that offered the impoverished an opportunity to improve their lives."

THE VISIONARY   *GEORGIA STATE BUILDING*

"When did all this happen?"

"Rachel, a Royal Charter was granted by King George II on June 6, 1732 to 21-trustees who would organize and govern the new colony. Oglethorpe was, it seems, the leading trustee. With the blessings of the King and funding from Parliament the new colony could elect its own governing board and enact its own laws and taxes."

"George II seemed generous."

"James, the King and Parliament were open to Oglethorpe's lobbying for the new colony for three reasons. First, the Crown wanted a buffer area between South Carolina and Spanish Florida and French Louisiana. Georgia would limit any Spanish or French northward aggression along the eastern seaboard. As a military man with a British Army commission Oglethorpe had served with distinction in numerous campaigns. He was the perfect person to govern the new colony given his army experience. Second, London's jails were full of debtors who hadn't paid their financial obligations. Reducing the number of people in jail was one way of removing an irritant, both financially and politically."

"I think I learned something about this in class, Martha. Weren't debtors put in jail until they paid what was owed?"

"Yes."

"But that makes no sense. How can you pay off your debts if you're in jail?"

"That was the paradox of the situation that Oglethorpe tried to remedy. He had served as the Chair of the Goals (Jail) Committee investigating London's debtor prisons. His report pointed out the absurdity of the situation and recommended a solution: a new colony for 'the worthy poor.' This became the second reason for establishing the colony. Of course, the third impulse was economic. The Trustees thought a silk industry could be established and perhaps a thriving wine business. These aspirations never worked out."

It was Mr. Freeman who asked the difficult question. "Martha, what about slavery?"

"Initially Georgia banned Black labor in the colony. Georgia, Oglethorpe believed, was not suited to grow rice and cotton where large-scale plantations would be needed, as existed in the Carolinas to the north. On the other hand, if a rice and silk economy could be established, there would be no need for large gangs of slaves. Though he was personally opposed to slavery, Oglethorpe had a less ethical reason for banning slavery. He felt slaves might unite with the Spanish in Florida to gain their freedom. This would counter the colony's position as a buffer between British and Spanish territories. He also felt that a slave system would have a negative effect on the morality of Georgia's white population. By its very nature slavery is a brutal, violent system of suppression and control that affects everyone, slave and taskmaster alike."

"But didn't Georgia end up with slavery anyway?"

"James?"

"That's what we learned in class."

"You're right. Oglethorpe did urge Parliament to ban slavery in the colony. In 1725 the House of Commons did just that. That decision did not sit well with many in the colony and some of the trustees who envied the slave prosperity of the Carolinas. The ban was ended in 1750."

"Always cash for flesh."

"Dad?"

"Just a thought, Martha. Let it pass."

Mr. Freeman

"As you know I didn't visit a state pavilion. I visited a vestige of the Spanish-American War of 1898, the Commonwealth of Puerto Rico. I always had an interest in the island, as your mother knows."

"Mom..."

"A little almost unknown piece of our family history. In the last days of the Reconstruction Era one member of our family on your dad's side decided to leave the harshness of Jim Crow Louisiana and KKK bigots riding through the countryside. He was light-skinned, so much so that he could pass as white if he dressed right and spoke in a low voice. He could read and write having gone to one year of high school, which was unusual at that time. He had also worked in the sugarcane fields and was quite knowledgeable about raising this crop. And one other thing... He could speak some French and Spanish. That happens when you grow up in New Orleans. Anyway, one day he boarded a passenger ship to the island hoping to find work."

"What happened to him?" Rachel asked.

"We're not sure. We have a few letters but that's it. Your father has always wanted to go to Puerto Rico to find Uncle Henry, as we call him."

"Dad, is that why you went to that venue?"

"In a word, yes."

_____

FAIR FACTS

Though it was not a state Puerto Rico was permitted venue space in the New York World's Fair. That decision was based on three things: first, the Puerto Ricans were citizens of the United States since 1917. They could move freely between the island and the mainland. Second, New York City had a sizeable Puerto Rican population that, it was hoped, would attend the Fair. Third, though the island's population could not vote in national elections, Puerto Ricans with American citizenship could. For these reasons the Fair Committee welcomed their Caribbean neighbor, located 1,000 miles from Miami, Florida, and sandwiched between the Dominican Republic and the US Virgin Islands.

THE ISLAND FLAG

———————

It was the inquisitive James who asked, "Why didn't Uncle Henry go north to Minnesota or Illinois, or even further to Canada like people did in the Underground Railroad?"

"We're not sure. Perhaps it was all about proximity and means of travel. Getting to the island was, I'm guessing, easier than traveling northward by land. Or maybe he thought a Black had a better shot where he might fit in easier, even if he could pass. In truth we'll never know for sure."

Uncle Henry… Another unsolved puzzle in the world of a migrating people, always with unanswered questions… Where was my ancestral home? How did I get to this place? Where should I go? Do I really have a home? Uncle Henry what are the answers? Why didn't you leave a diary?

"Dad, a couple of questions."

"Rachel?"

"I know that Christopher Columbus arrived on the island about 1493. Right?"

"Right."

"But didn't he name the island San Juan Bautista?"

"That's what I was told today. The name honored Saint John the Baptist. In time Puerto Rico was used after the United States acquired the island during the Spanish-American War of 1898. The Treaty of

Paris of that year made it all legal. Puerto Rico was Spanish for "rich port."

"I never understood that conflict," Martha said. "Dad, what was it all about?"

"I can only tell you what our guide said."

FAIR FACTS

The United States has always had an interest in the Caribbean to protect its eastern shoreline and southern coasts. Toward the turn of the century naval strategists were influenced by a little known book entitled, *The Influence of Sea Power Upon History*. The author was Captain Alfred Thayer Mahan. He argued a strong sea force was necessary for trade in peacetime and against enemies in wartime. As a model he referred to the British Navy. A large navy required coaling stations and naval bases, whether leased or acquired by force. Since the United States faced two bodies of water both an Atlantic and Pacific fleet were necessary, what he called a two-ocean navy. That, of course, meant transiting Terra del Fuego at the tip of Argentina, a demanding voyage in distance and time, if not rough weather. Was there an alternative? A canal through the Isthmus of Panama would permit ships to transit from one ocean to another. Assuming a canal was built, American control of strategic Caribbean islands would safeguard the vital installation. As a result of the war with Spain, the United States acquired Cuba and Puerto Rico. The stage was set for an American attempt to cut through the land, an effort that stymied the French de Lesseps' company.

THE CANAL

———————————————

"That's what I learned."

"The canal was quite a project."

"It was, James. It was very similar to building Hoover Dam. One cut a waterway through mountainous terrain, while the other impounded a massive lake. And now a question…"

Mr. Freeman had the look, which the family referred to as his "trickster face." He was up to something, that much they knew.

"Okay, which way does the canal run, north-south or east-west?"

"East-west," Rachel quickly blurted out, "from the Atlantic to the Pacific."

"I agree," Martha added. From the east coast of Panama to the west coast."

"James?"

"There's a trick here. The waters are on the east and west of Panama, but…"

"But?"

"Let me look at your map the guide gave you."

This Mr. Freeman did. In a moment James smiled, "Dad, the Canal runs north-south, from Colon to Panama City. Right?"

Mr. Freeman just smiled, as did his wife.

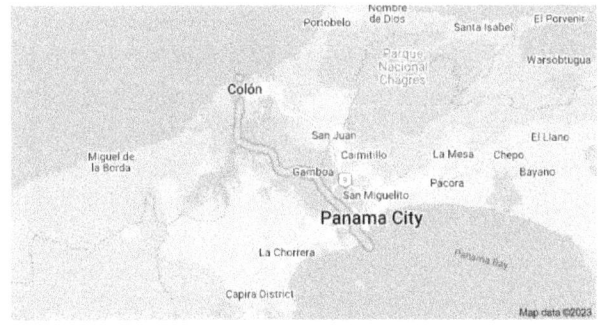

CHAPTER 20 – POSTCARDS

<u>That Night</u>

The Freemans were gathering around their dining room table. The dinner dishes were washed and put away. Roast beef and baked potatoes along with a sprinkling of green peas had been enjoyed. Given the hot weather ice tea with a slice of lemon had slackened their thirst. A home baked apple pie, still warm to the taste, awaited the family even as they prepared to share postcards they had bought at the Fair. It was a family ritual. Wherever they went each family member bought at least one postcard. They then talked about their card before placing them in a photo album. Mr. Freeman got things going.

<u>Mr. Freeman</u>

Holding up his card he said, "It will come to no one's surprise that I purchased this card. I guess I bought it for Uncle Henry. It portrays the Puerto Rico venue."

"And the other card, Dad?" Rachel asked.

"The Constitutional Mall. The aerial view was quite something. I think some refer to this as the 'God's eye view.'"

109—GENERAL VIEW. MAIN EXHIBIT AREA.

THE CONSTITUTIONAL MALL

Rachel

Holding up her first card she said, "I liked the simplicity and beauty of this card. It just reminded me of all the good times we've had, all the things we've seen. The artist's drawing of the lady flying through the sky really got to me."

"And the other card, Rachel?"

"Mom, I couldn't resist it. The sculpture of all those frogs jumping around in the pond really tickled me. And the great beast splashing in the water reminded me of a water buffalo I once saw in a movie."

Martha

"My first card, I must confess, was really a poster that called out to me. The woman with her arm held high with a glowing smile was so appealing. She seemed so happy, so full of life… And anyway, as you all know blue is my favorite color. My other postcard illustrated the *Bridge of Wings* that connected different venues. The wings, of course, are the flags representing all the countries participating in the Fair. Unfurled and floating in the air they did remind me of winged-creatures."

Mrs. Freeman

"I did like this card. It depicts a model home outside of the city in the City of Tomorrow. There's lots of greenery and not just paved streets and high-rise apartments. People aren't crowded together. Wouldn't that be a nice place to live and to raise kids?"

Model Homes in the Town of Tomorrow, New York World's Fair

"My other favorite is this. The New York World's Fair is greeting people from all over the world and, I would like to think, our family. Anyway, I liked the way the Fair venues were placed in the large letters."

James

"This card really got to me. It took me awhile to figure out what's going on. The rider, sort of like a Greek god, is riding a horse of awesome power. The statue symbolized the rapidity with which human thoughts may be transmitted through space by means of television, radio, and telegraph."

"My other cards, I found irresistible, a lady parachuting into the World's Fair. That's cool."

––––––––––––

FAIR FACTS

Postcards were an important part of the New York World's Fair. Visitors bought them to share with people back home the great time they were having in New York. They also purchased them as keepsakes, reminding one and all of the sights they saw. Naturally, the cards also ended up in photo albums since even the new Kodak cameras had a difficult time keeping up with professional photographers. Postcards also played another role, one less obvious to visitors. They were a source of commercial advertising for participating companies at the Fair. For example:

WONDER BREAD

ELGIN WATCH

US STEEL

THE NEW BUICK

Seemingly there was a postcard for every attraction and sometimes the venue itself was the artistic attraction that drew, "Will you look at that?" comments.

THE MERCURY CAR *THE FORD MOTOR COMPANY VENUE*

THE CANADIAN VENUE *THE NEW YORK WORLD'S FAIR MEDAL*

Once the family had completed sharing postcards Mr. Freeman had so say what was on their minds.

"Tomorrow is our last day at the Fair."

"We're meeting with Augusta?"

"Absolutely, Rachel. She's our guide. Tomorrow we focus on art and that's her thing. It should be a good day."

"The days have gone by so quickly," Martha said. "So very quickly."

"But what a time we've had."

"Rachel, of course, you're right. I just wanted it to continue a little longer."

"We have our memories, all the things we saw and all the things we've learned. And don't forget… We did it without breaking the bank."

"Which as the father of this family I did appreciate."

Mr. Freeman now turned to James, saying, "Any last thoughts?"

"Statues and art, I guess I'll survive."

CHAPTER 21 – A LIVING MUSEUM

DAY 6 – JULY 28, 1940

The Freeman family arrived at the Fair prepared for a long day and a few hours into the evening. Their last day at the New York World's Fair would, they hoped, be memorable. How could it not be? Augusta Savage was going to escort them through what she called "a living museum." Not only that… She would also explain what they were looking at and something about the artists behind the plaster and bronze. It would be, they expected, day one of their own art appreciation class. It would be a final way to end their days at the New York World's Fair.

Augusta was waiting for them in front of the Helicline where excited visitors were moving from the Perisphere to the Trylon. She wore a colorful dress exhibiting a rainbow of bright reds, blues, and yellows dominating flowers of all descriptions, a sort of sparkling garden on the move. Over one shoulder was an extra-large purse. She met them with a bright smile and hugs for all.

"What a beautiful dress," Rachel exclaimed. "Where did you get it?"

"Not at Sears, I'm afraid."

"Macys?" Martha asked.

"It's a one of a kind."

"Let me guess," Mrs. Freeman said. "You bartered again. Art lessons for a sewing genius, right?"

"Bartering does have its advantages."

"I think you look just great," James announced a bit shyly. "Simply terrific."

"Well, thank you young man. Your compliment is most appreciated."

"Perhaps your bartering seamstress would consider free garbage collection for a month, or music lessons from my wife for another swap?"

"I'll check out your proposal."

The chitchat was over. It was time for art.

Art Stop #1

"This is our first stop."
"We've been here before when we walked the Helicline, Augusta."
"True, James."
"So?"
"While your attention was on other things you missed *The Astronomer.*"
"What?"
"Look over to the left, James."

This James did.

"How did I miss that statue? It's gigantic."
"At thirty feet tall, gigantic applies."
"It's so striking." Martha said. "The male body, so beautiful."
"And no clover leafs you-know-where," Rachel added with a sensuous grin. "Not like the Church fathers covering up those wonderful statues in Rome."

THE ASTRONOMER

"What's that in his hand?" Mr. Freeman asked in his usual straightforward way. "Could it be the Earth? Or the solar system?"

"Perhaps both."

"I think it's all of creation," James said. "You know, the powers beyond our understanding, what some people refer to as god."

All turned to James with various looks of amazement. What was happening? James was evolving right before their eyes, from comic books to thoughts philosophical in nature.

Augusta broke the momentary spell, saying, "Let me tell you a little about the artist, Carl Milles."

CARL MILLES

"He is a Swedish sculptor and architect. He's best known for his large-scale fountains that according to the critics were both expressive and rhythmical. He studied in France and was influenced by the French romantic sculptor Auguste Rodin. Milles worked in clay (for casting into bronze). He also worked with stone and wood. I have pictures of two of his most famous efforts."

Augusta reached into her handbag and pulled out two photographs. The sisters immediately took to *The Female Dancers*, while Mrs. Freeman looked with awe at *The Hand of God*.

THE FEMALE DANCERS *THE HAND OF GOD*

Art Stop #2

 Led by Augusta the Freeman family followed her into the
Produce and Distribution Zone where they stopped before the beautiful
Dances of the Races. It stood in front of the building for New York City.
There she told them that the sculpture by Malvina Hoffman depicted
the world of dance as seen among the various cultural groups around
the world. This was appropriate since her commission by the Fair was to
sculpt a work dealing with the human races. In preparation for this and
other work Hoffman had spent two years traveling around the world to
see and experience the variety of dance traditions on every continent.

DANCES OF THE RACES

THE ARTIST AND HER WORK

"Augusta, thank you for showing this to us."

"It's my pleasure, Rachel."

"It seems like everyone in the world loves to dance," Martha added. "And there are so many ways to do so."

"That's what Hoffman was trying to show, a kind of equality of cultures, at least when it came to dance."

"Where to now?" James asked.

"To your favorite place, the Amusement Zone."

Art Stop #3

"Would you look at that?" Mr. Freeman said. "This art you should like, James."

"Dad, I can run fast on the track, even jump a bit, but throw a hunk of metal, no way. This guy looks like he could win an Olympic medal."

What had caught their eye was Raoul Josset's *The Shot Putter*. Almost immediately James made an unusual connection.

"*The Astronomer* and *The Shot Putter* are like twins, one holding creation in his hands, the other seeking athletic prowess, as if he were seeking the limit of human skill and energy."

Again, the family stared at the young man, as if to say, "Who is this person? One minute ago he was infatuated with Superman and now he's gushing philosophy."

Augusta suddenly walked over to James and embraced him, saying, "There seems to be more to you than we assumed." James, somewhat embarrassed by the moment, could only smile.

THE SHOT PUTTER

"I know little about Josset beyond this. During the Great War he worked as an interpreter for American forces in France. He was also a pupil of Antoine Bourdelle in the 1920's before coming to the United States. I do have, however, a photograph of one of his best efforts, at least in my opinion. It's called *The Spirit of the Centennial* to celebrate the Texas Centennial Exposition. As you will see it's quite something. Notice that it commemorates the role of women in the history of Texas."

THE SPIRIT OF THE CENTENNIAL

Art Stop #4

The next stop was at the Special Events Center in the Community Interests Zone by the Hall of Fashion. Once there Augusta told the family about Robert Foster's unique work, *Textiles*.

"He took sheets of steel for this work. He electrically welded and bent the sheets to the artistic shape in his mind. The result was what some call 'a heroic-sized surrealistic figure symbolizing textiles.' Isn't it something?"

"Augusta, has he shaped a woman?" Mrs. Freeman asked.
"Some say that."

"Wouldn't that go along with textiles, cloth, wool, all the things women use to make garments and blankets?"

"Again, Rachel, some might reach that interpretation."

"Whatever," Martha said. "But just look at the flowing lines. The whole figure seems to float in air."

"Mr. Freeman, no comment?"

"I'm at a loss for words beyond admiring the craftsmanship with metal."

"And you, James?"

"It reminds me of the Tin Man in the *Wizard of Oz*, but in this case no oil is needed and the wicked witch is nowhere to be seen."

"I'll take that to mean you like it?"

"I do."

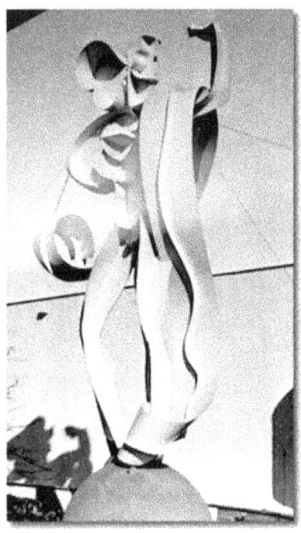

TEXTILES

Art Stop #5

Augusta led her newly acquired family back to the Amusement Zone where they stopped in front of Times Square. There they grouped among a throng of visitors, most of who were gawking at a statue entitled *Wings*. Of course, none of them had an Augusta Savage to explain a few things.

"This sculpture is composed of three enormous wings. They flow from the backs of figures of man and a woman. I'm told that the work provides an impressionist symbol of man's future in the sky."

WINGS

"I love it."

"Martha?"

"Augusta, the statue seems ready to take flight."

"I think it's already airborne," James added. "It reminds me of the paper airplanes I used to make with Dad. You know... Fold here, bend there, and throw with thrust. I feel like I could do that with *Wings*."

"Well, if Lindbergh could fly the Atlantic, I guess anything is possible."

"Did you say the sculpture was done by Gertrude Vanderbilt, Augusta?"

"I did, Rachel."

"That name seems familiar."

"It should be. She has a pedigree background. She is the daughter of Cornelius Vanderbilt II and a great-granddaughter of Commodore Cornelius Vanderbilt. She is also the founder of the Whitney Museum of American Art in New York City. It is a wonderful museum. I highly recommend a visit."

"With her wealthy background she still went into the competitive art world?"

"That she did, Rachel. Her work as a sculptor is to be admired. She is also a noted patron of the arts and, given her resources, a collector of great renown."

"Can she help you to save *The Harp*?"

"Mr. Freeman, yes she could."

"But?"

"No offers yet from her."

Art Stop #6

Walking in her wake the Freemans followed Augusta into the Food Zone and to the Heinz Pavilion. There they saw a decorative fountain designed by Raymond Barger. It was called the *Sea Maid*. Those in the art world described it as "amusing" and intended to "harmonize with the landscape."

"I believe this is his first major commission. What do you think of it?"

"Augusta, it's so playful, almost childlike."

"Martha, perhaps it is. Rachel, your thoughts?"

"His work reminds me of a mermaid, half fish, half human."

"And, James, what do you think?"

Of course, James, as always, surprised all with his response. "If you fall in love with a mermaid, where do you live?"

James' parents smiled, his sisters gave each other sisterly looks while Augusta found herself bemused by the young man's observation. Where indeed would they live? For a fleeting moment the question turned unexpectedly on her, leaving her unable to avoid it. Where and how should Blacks live? Were they really a part of the society, or simply some incarnation, not wholly of America, nor of Africa? These thoughts she kept to herself as she said, "On to the next stop."

SEA MAID *THE SCULPTOR*

Art Stop #7

The migrating group now stopped in front of what was called the largest sundial in the world. Made of white plaster the sundial was 80 feet tall. Paul Manship was commissioned by the New York World's Fair to create this work. According to the artist, "The Perisphere and the Trylon at the World's Fair suggested to me measurements of time and space, so my sundial relates to the background of the central motif of the Fair." His work was entitled *Time and Fates of Man*. It stood in front of the Perisphere and the Trylon.

Time and Fates of Man

Holding up the sundial's pointer was a tree. Sitting on the tree were the "three fates," sometimes referred to as *The Daughters of Necessity* from Greek mythology. All this Augusta explained to the Freemans.

"I know about this," Rachel said. "I took a class in world mythologies."

"And what did you learn about the *Daughters*?"

"Augusta, Themis was the Goddess of Necessity. The three women were the children of Themis and Zeus. Each one symbolizes an aspect of life. They were known as *The Fates*. Life was woven by Clotho. Life was measured by Lachesis. The thread of life was ended by Atrapos. All human beings are influenced by these mythological deities. All life must submit to these divine daughters."

"Now I understand why Manship did this."

"Augusta?"

"Rachel, from what I know he consistently created mythological pieces in what is called the 'Classical style.'"

"Well, he certainly lived up to his reputation with *Time and Fates of Man*."

"And maybe countries, Augusta."

"Meaning what, James?"

"Standing in the background is the giant statue of George Washington. I was just wondering."

"Yes?"

"Do the *Fates* influence countries?"

THE FATES

Art Stop #8

Keeping up with Augusta was providing the Freeman family with all the physical exercise they needed. The woman seemed to be in perpetual motion, always darting this way and that through the ever-increasing crowds. The longitude and latitude of her obvious planning now brought everyone to the Consumer Building in the Production and Distribution Zone. There they stopped before a statue called *Labors of Man*, a work completed by George H. Snowden. Here, Augusta explained what they were looking at.

"The work is in three parts. In the first part man is employing his mind to carve out his destiny. In the second section he attempts to control nature in order to build a civilization. In the last part, he deals with his own savage nature that knows no bounds when it comes to acts of evil. That's at least how I see it."

EMPLOYING THE HUMAN MIND   *CONTROLLING NATURE*

CONQUERING EVIL

"I wonder…"

"Mr. Freeman?"

"This business about controlling nature… I'm not sure about that. I mean, think of the 'dust bowls' sweeping across the Great Plains, all that top soil blown into the sky due to overuse of the land. Or the floods along the Mississippi River regardless of the earthen embankments to protect homes and farms … Or the pollution of the Great Lakes due to toxic waste drained into those once pristine lakes…"

"That's why dams are important."

"James?"

"Flood control… Hydroelectric power… Reservoirs of clean drinking water… You know, like Boulder Dam and the stuff they're building on the Tennessee River with that TVA project."

221

"You learned that in class, too?"

"My teacher supports the New Deal programs. He wants us to be aware of them and, I guess, to consider voting for FDR in 1944 if he runs a fourth time."

"Why not in 1940?"

"Simple. I'll be a high school graduate and old enough for the draft, but not for the vote. I've got to wait until I'm 21."

"Let's turn to this business about evil. Mrs. Freeman?"

"Augusta, the serpent carved by Snowden is a constant reminder of the potential evilness lurking in all of us. It's a fulltime job to avoid hating, to avoid bigotry, to avoid scapegoating... And most of all to avoid war... We see it everyday in the papers, even the movies. Good versus evil... Darkness challenging the light... Anger overwhelming forgiveness... And it affects all of us, even good Christians like our family."

Whatever the intent of Snowden's work, Mrs. Freeman's voice rang with simple clarity. As human beings, we have the capacity to love or to devour each other in an orgy of personal vengeance. She then turned to her children, saying in unbridled words, "No matter what awful things you experience as a Black person, always maintain your dignity and never spit back in anger. Remain peaceful and, supported by your faith, find a way to change your oppressor. Use your mind, not your fists. You know, like that fellow in India."

"Mahatma Gandhi?"

"Yes, James."

"Like the first business... Using your mind to control your destiny?"

"Yes."

In her mind, Augusta Savage had an interesting thought that swirled around seeking expression. "Snowden has created a fascinating 'trinity' all of his own, yet one universal in its meaning."

Art Stop #9

After a meal on the run at a diner specializing in New York white sausage, rather than the usual hot Bronx dogs, the Freemans continued to follow Augusta. It should be noted that the sausage was covered with heaps of yellow mustard and layers of sparkling green relish in contrast to a generous sprinkling of chopped white onions. All this was, of course, enjoyed with Atlanta's favorite drink, a crisp, carbonated *Coca Cola* with plenty of ice.

Augusta called a halt once they got to the Court of Power in the Government Zone. Before them was a statue by John Gregory entitled *The Four Victories of Peace*. The work consisted of four female figures representing *Wheels, Wings, Wheat,* and *Wisdom*.

THE FOUR VICTORIES OF PEACE

"I must admit I know little about the sculptor or what he wanted the public to appreciate. However, the work is so beautifully done. I certainly didn't want you to miss it. I'm afraid it's up to us to provide personal interpretations. James?"

"Two things stand out immediately. First, there are four women portrayed. Second, the things they symbolize all begin with the letter W. I think that's called alliteration."

"Anything else, Rachel?"

"The W's refer to positive aspects of life in the absence of war. It's tough to grow wheat with tanks crashing through fertile farmland."

"Mrs. Freeman?"

"Women bear children. They bring life into this world. That is why, I think, four women are shown. They are about nourishing life and transmitting wisdom from one generation to another."

"Martha?"

"Wheels and wings… This is about transporting the bounty of our farms to the cities. Without our farms there can be no life in heavily populated areas."

"James?"

"The word 'victories' intrigues me. The W's are alluding to the fruits of peace in contrast to destruction and killing, all those terrible things that happen in war."

"Mr. Freeman?"

"I think Gregory was offering us a stark choice, war or peace? I believe he was considering the current world situation. Europe has a choice, war or peace. The same is true for Japan. Eventually our own country will have to decide, war or peace. He was pointing out to us what we have to lose if war overtakes us. And now, Augusta, what do you think?"

"I am intrigued by all your comments. I find myself in general agreement and I must say you all make for fine art students."

Art Stop #10

"This is our last stop."

"Thankfully, Augusta, my shoe leather is about worn out."

"Here, Mrs. Freeman, just sit on this bench with your husband. The children are strong. They can stand."

Augusta had brought the family to a statue of Walt Whitman. It was located on the edge of the Perylon Court, midway between Perylon Hall and the Perisphere. It was, she told them, one of the few non-plaster sculptures at the Fair. It was bronze, she pointed out, a much more durable material.

"This work is called by two names, *The Open Road* or *Afoot and Lighthearted*. You can decide which you prefer."

WALT WHITMAN

"As you know Walt Whitman was an American poet, essayist, and journalist. Perhaps you've read a few verses from his monumental work, *Leaves of Grass*? And again perhaps you're wondering why this is our last stop? Certainly Jo Davidson has provided a remarkable statue of a great American. No question about that. However, beyond the artistic value of the work, I have something else in mind."

Augusta then reached into her large purse and brought out six sheets of paper. She handed each member of the family a sheet face down, requesting that they not peek.

"During the past few days I have developed an affection for you. In a way you have become a surrogate family. I have often listened with interest as you commented on the pavilions and, of course, on today's forced march through thick crowds to view the living art of this Fair. And now we are here before Walt Whitman. Obviously, it is not by chance. During our short time together, a shadow has followed us, which as Blacks we could not elude. Racial issues have been our traveling companions."

Augusta now stopped to compose herself. Then going on she said, "James, you in particular have asked troubling and penetrating questions. All of you have responded to his inquisitive mind with your own questions and commentary. Since I too share our common Black history, both the joy and harshness of it, I wanted to leave you with a gift on this, your last day at the New York World's Fair. What I have bequeathed will, I hope, help all of us in the days ahead for I too want to live in a world shed of racial prejudice. Now, please turn over your sheets."

This everyone did. What they found came as a surprise. Augusta had made copies of Walt Whitman's elegant poem to a fallen president, *O Captain! My Captain*. Gathering all in a close circle she said, "There is joy and sorrow in this poem, but there is also hope that can sustain us as a people and a country. Consider the opening stanza."

> *O Captain! My Captain! Our fearful trip is done.*
> *The ship has weather'd every rack, the prize we sought is won.*
> *The port is near, the bells I hear, the people all exulting.*
> *While follow eyes the steady keel, the vessel grim and daring;*
> *But O heart! heart! heart!*
> *O the bleeding drops of red,*
> *Where on the deck my Captain lies,*
> *Fallen cold and dead.*

"I find these lines inspirational. President Abraham Lincoln, a good man, was torn from us even in the moment of victory over the Confederacy. His and our fateful trip was done. The Union was victorious. Slavery was ended. The great prize of the war was achieved. Our country would have a new birth of freedom. Even as the people cried in despair at the loss of their Captain, they also exalted at the bells of freedom and the hope of a more just Union of all Americans. These few lines I hold dear, as I do you. I trust they will inspire and sustain you through the years to come. Please know I am most blessed to have wandered into your lives."

The ship has weather'd every rack, the prize we sought is won.

LEGACIES

<u>The Freeman Family</u>

It appears that...

Mr. Freeman retired in 1950 from his garbage-hauling job with New York City. He went away with a nice gold watch to celebrate his many years of devoted work. In retirement he donated time to mentoring young boys in Harlem through the local YMCA. As he had with his son James, he tried to keep these boys focused on their education and staying out of trouble. He also took up a hobby. He constructed small scale trains in his garage and then ran them on a large sheet of plywood, the tracks moving though small towns and across the landscape. It wasn't quite what he had seen at the New York World's Fair, but it was enough. Every Saturday he invited the neighborhood kids to watch his trains. Of course, he always wore his B and O engineer's hat when he did so. He and his family still live in their small home in Harlem.

Mrs. Freeman retired two years before her husband from the New York Public Schools. She was given quite a sendoff from many of her former students. She was also given a nice plaque from the school district and a Certificate of Appreciation from the local ward boss. Almost immediately she turned her attention toward the developing civil rights movement enveloping the Black community. That meant getting really involved with the local Urban League and the NAACP. She quickly emerged as the secretary in the local chapters of these organizations. When not involved she mentored children with reading deficiencies, as well as kids interested in learning to play the piano. Once a month she took out her Japanese tea set when hosting her book club.

Rachel went to Columbia University after finishing two years at City College of New York. There she completed an English major with an emphasis on British Literature and the other man in her life, one William Shakespeare. Prodded by her professors she stayed on at Columbia and eventually received her Ph.D. That in hand she ventured across the country where she landed at San Francisco State. In time she received tenure and soon after met a handsome assistant professor. Marriage followed and in time two kids. Currently she is writing children's books that introduce youthful readers to the "Bard." All this she did when not protesting for the end of segregationist practices in housing in South San Francisco where she and her husband had bought a home over the strident objections of many.

Martha continued her studies in Economics. After graduation from Syracuse University she went to work for Westinghouse while living in Long Island. In time, she married a great guy who was an accountant but also a law graduate. And yes, he also worked at Westinghouse. They have three kids. Together they started a small business to bring a necessary service to the Black community. They helped folks with their income tax returns, investments, and dealing with unreasonable landlords. In their own way, they were a part of the civil rights movement.

Now, as to James… No basketball scholarship came his way. The young man attended a small college in Brooklyn on a modest academic scholarship, taking math and science classes with thoughts of being an engineer. In his senior year he turned his sights on law and worked his way through a small law school in upstate New York that was partial to assisting people of color. Once he passed his state bar examination he headed west, settling in Denver and immediately going to work for the local NAACP as a civil rights attorney. He's not married but does enjoy the company of a terrific gal from Boise, Idaho. Oh, yes, James did visit Boulder Dam. He is considered quite an expert on that beautifully curved slab of cement.

As you would expect the Freemans have maintained their relationship with Augusta Savage. And, why not, she was family.

Augusta Savage

Once the New York World's Fair closed Augusta Savage went on with her work, though commissions were less frequent after Pearl Harbor. Following the war she continued what was now her life's work to teach young Black artists how to sculpt, draw, and paint. She also helped establish the Harlem Artist Guild that created career opportunities for young artists, while promoting civil rights activism through art. In doing so she believed her legacy would live on with the work of her students. One of her students was Charles Alston who did a bust of Martin Luther King Jr. This was the first work of a Black artist to be placed in the White House.

In 1946, Augusta Savage made a major decision. She moved from Harlem to Saugerties, New York to be closer to her daughter, Irene. There she bought a farmhouse in need of major repairs. There she raised chickens and pigeons to sell in NYC. She also took care of mice in the cancer research lab of Herman Knaust in exchange for her beloved clay. Beyond that she also turned the existing chicken coup into a sculpture studio and classroom for aspiring artists. Late in life, she moved in with her daughter. On March 26, 1962 she died of cancer. She was 70-years old. In 1999, Karlyn Knaust Elia purchased the Saugerties home and restored it for the exhibition of Augusta Savage's works. Karlyn was the granddaughter of Herman Knaust. The house is now listed on the New York State and the National Register of Historic Places as the *Augusta Savage House and Studio*. Much later the State of Florida did the same for her place of birth in Green Cove Springs.

THE FARMHOUSE

In 1935 Augusta Savage stated her own legacy, telling *Metropolitan Magazine:*

I have created nothing really beautiful, really lasting, but if I can inspire one of these youngsters to develop the talent I know they possess, then my monument will be their work.

In 1939, she produced one of her most telling works. It was called *Realization.* It showed a Black couple crouched in oppression, holding onto each other at the auction block, stripped of their clothing and dignity. But *Realization* portrays more than this. It is also about what can be, a day when slavery would end, a day when all Americans would be treated equally before the law. That long trek would not be easy but it was one Augusta Savage took to her everlasting glory.

REALIZATION

Augusta Savage was buried in the Ferncliff Cemetery and Mausoleum in Hartsdale, Westchester County, New York. Her personal papers are housed in the Schomburg Center for Research and Black Culture at the New York City Public Library.